WHERE HAVE ALL THE VOTERS GONE?

Other Norton volumes by Everett Carll Ladd, Jr.

AMERICAN POLITICAL PARTIES

IDEOLOGY IN AMERICA: CHANGE AND RESPONSE
IN A CITY, A SUBURB, AND A SMALL TOWN

THE DIVIDED ACADEMY: PROFESSORS AND POLITICS
(with Seymour Martin Lipset)

TRANSFORMATIONS OF THE AMERICAN PARTY SYSTEM
(with Charles D. Hadley)

Where Have All the Voters Gone?

☆ ☆ ☆ ☆ ☆ ☆ ☆ ☆ ☆ ☆ ☆ ☆ ☆ ☆ ☆

The Fracturing of America's Political Parties

by

EVERETT CARLL LADD, JR.

W·W·NORTON & COMPANY·INC·
New York

Library of Congress Cataloging in Publication Data
Ladd, Everett Carll, Jr.
  Where have all the voters gone?
  Includes index.
  1. Political parties—United States.   I. Title.
JK2261.L343   329'.02   78–17595
ISBN 0–393–05691–0
ISBN 0–393–09011–6 pbk.

book designed by Jacques Chazaud
Set in Bulmer Italic and Caledonia
Typesetting by PennSet
Manufacturing by Murray Printing

1 2 3 4 5 6 7 8 9 0

For
Benjamin Elliot Ladd
with love

☆ ☆ ☆ ☆ ☆ ☆

Contents

Preface   ix

Introduction: A Party System in Decline   xiii

CHAPTER 1 The Unmaking of the Republican Party   1

CHAPTER 2 The Divided Democrats   26

CHAPTER 3 The Perils of Party Reform   50

Postscript   74

Index   79

☆ ☆ ☆ ☆ ☆ ☆

Preface

*E*ARLY IN 1977, ROBERT LUBAR, THE MANAGING EDITOR OF *Fortune*, invited me to write a series of three articles for his magazine on the current condition of the American party system. I accepted, and whatever merit the present volume has owes much to that invitation and to the subsequent encouragement and support which Bob Lubar provided. The articles appeared in the September, October, and November 1977 issues of *Fortune*. Somewhat expanded, these three articles comprise the core of the present volume.

On assignment for *Fortune*, I had an opportunity to supplement and otherwise modify my approach to the study of American political parties in two ways that seem important to me. First, I was able to interview about one hundred prominent public figures. Most of them came from the ranks of national party leadership—members of Congress, national committee members, candidates and aides to candidates in recent presidential elections—but some were state party officials, and others were prominent representatives of groups such as business and labor that have long occupied privileged positions within the two main parties. These interviews, guided by a general set of concerns but open and free-wheeling, offered me a number of insights into the current problems and performance of the U.S. parties. Almost without exception, the leaders whom I sought to interview agreed to meet with me, gave generously of their time, and spoke freely and forcefully. I owe these men and women a substantial debt, much more than is suggested by the specific citations in this volume.

My work for *Fortune* proved helpful in another, quite different, regard. I was enjoined to pay special attention to the consequences of the partisan phenomena I was describing for the overall performance of the American governmental system. There are two fundamentally different reasons for closely examining American political parties. In one of these—and this has characterized most of my past work on the topic—the observer is primarily concerned with understanding *conflict* in the country. The parties are alliances of social groups, and the ever-changing configurations of group loyalties reveal so many basic elements of social and political conflict. The other perspective—that of this volume—is quite different. Instead of looking *through* parties as windows to the society one looks *at* them as primary political institutions and asks how well they are performing.

I should note that this volume has benefited from an approach and from information which I have called upon in many past instances. The rich survey collection on American public opinion and orientations toward the parties has again proved especially useful. I was able to draw on an extensive body of Gallup survey data made available by the Gallup Organization through the Roper Center; on the surveys of Yankelovich, Skelly, and White, which are deposited at the Social Science Data Center of the University of Connecticut; on the General Social Surveys of the National Opinion Research Center of the University of Chicago; and on the national election surveys of the Center for Political Studies of the University of Michigan. There really are instances when the whole is more than the sum of its parts. The development of data archives in the social sciences, through which an investigator can tap literally hundreds of separate studies of the American populace, reaching back from the present time to the time of Franklin Delano Roosevelt, permits a type of analysis more sensitive to the complexities of public performance and to the changing patterns of partisan attachments than would be possible if all these individual studies were not part of an integrated research collection.

A good many people have contributed to this volume, and I welcome this opportunity to acknowledge their help. Seymour Martin Lipset and Austin Ranney, two colleagues and friends, commented on specific arguments which I presented and guided me away from at least some of the errors of interpretation to which I was inclined. More importantly, perhaps, their own extensive scholarship in areas related to this work has contributed to the development of the more general perspectives which I offer.

A number of staff members of the Social Science Data Center assisted in this project, in areas as diverse as the initial location of pertinent surveys, the preparation of data for computer analysis, and the demanding task of organizing information first for interpretation and subsequently for presentation. I want to thank in particular Diane L. Reed, assistant director for sponsored research at the center; Anne-Marie Mercure, assistant director for the archive; Eleanor S. Wilcox, my administrative assistant; Dana Suszkiw, my secretary, who so very ably prepared the final manuscripts; and Sally A. Daniels, Robert Keith MacDonald, Evelyn Vanden Dolder, Karen Shirghio, Kathleen J. Kowalyshyn, Joffre R. Levesque, Barbara S. Bentley, Margaret M. Pyne, John Devine, and Barry P. Warren— research associates and technical services personnel at the data center.

A special note of appreciation is due Rosalind Klein Berlin, a research associate at *Fortune,* who worked with me for eight months as the three original articles moved from initial conception to publication. Her good judgment and her hard work were, quite literally, essential to the completion of the project.

I benefited immeasurably from an association with two outstanding editors. At *Fortune,* Paul H. Weaver guided me through the series, never hesitating to tell me when he thought my thinking was muddled nor when he believed it to be sound, and forcefully intruded upon the presentation of my arguments while never once forgetting that, ultimately, the arguments had to be my own. At Norton, I have once again had the delight and the privilege of working with Donald S. Lamm. Only the two of us can know how much my work has benefited from his critical judgment and his continuing encouragement.

Most of the research for this book was completed while I was in residence at the Hoover Institution, Stanford University. The Institution provided a most supportive research environment. I owe a very special debt to Anne Connors Diesel, who was my administrative assistant and secretary at Hoover. She assisted in every phase of the research, with intelligence, perseverance, and a never-failing tolerance of a somewhat difficult author.

With all this recognition, only appropriately, being paid, it may fairly be asked what role I played. Just enough, it may be said, so that I alone must bear responsibility for any and all errors of interpretation or judgment which these pages may contain.

E.C.L.
Mansfield Depot, Connecticut
January 23, 1978

☆ ☆ ☆ ☆ ☆ ☆

A Party System in Decline

*I*N OCTOBER 1977 I SHARED WITH A GROUP OF CIVIC LEADERS many of the complaints about the current condition of the U.S. parties which are developed in this volume. Near the end of the discussion that followed my presentation, one member of the audience politely but pointedly inquired: "Do you really think that the American political system functioned better in the past than it does now, that everything is in decline?"

No, I don't. In many ways, the U.S. social and political system is now doing a better job responding to the needs of the entire citizenry than at any time in the past.

The fact remains, however, that Americans now feel notably dissatisfied with their primary public institutions. And this dissatisfaction—coming in the face of substantial achievements —seems to result in large measure from a breakdown in one critical institution designed to translate public expectations into public policy: the political parties. It is the argument of this volume that over the past decade and a half the parties have manifested a diminished capability. The party system is not functioning well. It is not doing a good job in performing those tasks which are uniquely its own. This failure carries with it serious consequences for popular confidence in the governing system.

Public Confidence and Public Life

A stream of opinion surveys attests to the fact that large numbers of Americans are unhappy with the performance of the principal institutions of their society—president and Congress, the courts, the press, business and labor, education and religion. Pollster Louis Harris has reported that a pronounced decline in popular satisfaction with the leadership of all of these institutions occurred between 1966 and 1974. And even with Vietnam and Watergate behind us, according to Harris, there has been only a limited recovery of popular "confidence" since the dark and angry "Watergate Summer" of 1974.* Congress was held in high confidence, for example, by 42 percent of Americans in 1966, but was so esteemed by just 15 percent of the public at the end of 1977.

While other survey explorations yield findings that vary somewhat from those of Harris, their basic conclusion is the same.†

This diminished public satisfaction, like most complex phenomena, has invited a number of explanations. Some observers have detected a vast extension of an "adversary style," whereby every problem or problematic condition comes to be

---

* *The Harris Survey Yearbook of Public Opinion*, 1971, p. 60; *The Harris Survey*, October 6, 1973; March 22, 1976; March 14, 1977; and January 5, 1978.

† For a detailed review of these data, see Ladd, "The Polls: The Question of Confidence," *The Public Opinion Quarterly* (Winter 1976–1977), pp. 544–52; and "The Matter of Public Confidence: Inadequate Data and Untested Theories," a paper presented at the 1977 meeting of the American Association for Public Opinion Research, Buck Hill Falls, Pennsylvania, May 19–22, 1977.

depicted as a scandal, an outrage, or a crisis. In particular, the national press has adopted ever more sharply over the last decade an adversary approach vis-à-vis the other principal institutions of the system, exposing, even dramatizing their failures. Public awareness of inadequacy in performance is thus raised.* For others, the key involves a mushrooming growth of political utopianism in the contemporary U.S. The American sociopolitical setting increasingly encourages heightened, unrealistic expectations as to what performance standards social institutions can attain.†

My own interpretation, buttressed by considerable rummaging in survey data, is that the dissatisfaction we are witnessing owes much to a factor more direct and straightforward—to the widespread sense within the populace that this is an unusually fortunate and well-endowed society that is currently manifesting considerable difficulty in responding effectively to public problems. When Americans contemplate their own personal situation and that of their families, they find considerable cause for satisfaction. When they consider the fundamental organization of their society, as in the arrangement of government and the economy, they see no valid claim for drastic change. Indeed, they strongly defend the established order. But they believe that the primary institutions of the society, rather than making the most of the generally fortunate situation in which the country finds itself, are through various sundry shortcomings detracting from it.

In particular, the governmental engine is sputtering. It has not broken down. There is hardly any public enthusiasm for

---

* Paul A. Weaver, "Do the American People Know What They Want?" *Commentary* (December 1977), pp. 62–67.

† This point is argued forcefully by Irving Kristol. See his *On the Democratic Idea in America* (New York: Harper and Row, 1972), especially pp. 127–49. See, too, Ben J. Wattenberg, *The Real America* (Garden City, N.Y.: Doubleday, 1974).

scrapping it. It has not been used for pernicious tasks. But it just does not run smoothly. It does not merit a high measure of public confidence.

The Party Failure

At the core of the performance problem to which the public is responding is the matter of *control* and *responsiveness*. Some measure of demoralization in public opinion is bound to occur in a democratic system when it is perceived that popular wishes or expectations are very imperfectly translated into institutional response. It can never be easy in a diverse, pluralistic nation of 215 million people to achieve a high measure of popular control over the main public institutions and the continuing responsiveness of these institutions to popular wishes. But, in our time, control and responsiveness have proved increasingly elusive, especially with the breakdown of an institution charged with their achievement, the political parties.

Parties are one component of the malperforming engine of governance in the United States. Their malfunction is surely not the only cause of the engine's sluggishness and the public's resulting unease. They are, however, an important part generally, and their responsibility for achieving popular control is especially large.

It is easy to lose sight of the fact that parties are *institutions* in the governing process, with responsibilities in many ways as imposing as those of legislatures, courts, and executive branches. The parties' institutional role involves serving as intermediaries between a mass public and the formal structures of the government.

The potential electorate in the United States (persons of voting age) now numbers about 150 million. There is no way so large a body can achieve the type of participation and control which democracy presupposes without a "linkage" institution that organizes and distills and translates. The party system retains exclusive custody of this core democratic function—of aggregating the preferences of the mass public for political leadership and policy choice, and converting what was incoherent and diffuse to specific, responsive public decisions.

Today, the parties simply are not doing a good job in this their primary area, and as a result, popular control and responsiveness suffer.

What Is Required?

We can understand the nature of the contemporary party failure in the U.S. a bit better if we examine the performance characteristics which are essential to success. Three are of central importance: *competing* in a sustained, structured, relatively even fashion; *representing* the populace, which requires a faithful response to the divisions within it and the reflection of those areas of broad agreement; and *organizing* both the electorate and the government so as to translate the diffuse policy expectations of the former into specific, appropriate actions by the latter.

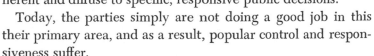

A Competitive System. Competition is important to the successful articulation of citizenry wishes through the party system, because voter discontent can be best expressed through support for a challenger to the "in" party. A party in power, knowing that it may be expelled if it does not perform, is more likely to attend to popular interests than one which has grown fat and complacent from a lack of challenge. The same general claims apply to party competition as to competition in the economy. The level of productivity is apt to be higher when the contending parties or producers feel their success or failure is dependent upon, in some significant measure, the job they do.

A competitive party situation is desirable from a standpoint of the trust and confidence of the electorate. It is nice to think one's vote matters. Sustained party competition increases the sense of electoral efficacy. When there is such competition, voters have reason to believe that they have a remedy in the event of shoddy performance by the incumbents.

Competition requires something more than the presence of a reasonably even balance among contending parties. It requires that the public be satisfied that the choice before them is a meaningful one—that the differences between the parties are those which really matter.

Finally, for competition to be effective it must be structured, arranged in terms of the overarching, integrative mechanism of party. There are so many different elective offices in a country like the U.S. that citizens cannot consider their votes meaningful instruments for *policy control* unless the myriad separate contests are linked up in some understandable fashion—unless, for instance, balloting for the 435 seats of a legislature can be seen as a struggle of one party against another, rather than unrelated, detached vying of individuals. Contests within a party, or any form of diffuse factionalism, are from the standpoint of popular control decidedly inferior to regular interparty rivalry.

An electoral system becomes truly competitive, then, when it provides easy opportunity for alternating "ins" and "outs," arranged as parties and not as individual candidates, and when its divisions are seen to mirror the salient conflicts of the society.

A Representative System. Parties are asked to engage in an extraordinary narrowing of the alternatives in the democratic struggle for public office. In contests for the presidency in the

U.S., for example, about 85 million people are now technically eligible to run (being at least thirty-five years of age and natural-born citizens), but only two individuals, typically, enter the general election with any chance of success. It is by no means automatic that most of the electorate will judge these profound reductions of the realistic alternatives to have been performed successfully. There is, obviously, a continuing problem of representativeness.

Ideal performance requires that each major party begin general election campaigns with candidates broadly representative of the wishes (involving style, policy perspectives, and the like) of those voters making up its "regular expected majority." To the extent that selection processes and mechanisms fail to produce nominees who reflect the *coalitional* character of each party, and instead advantage sectors of the party with special, exclusive interests or particularistic candidate preferences, the ability to be representative is diminished and the responsiveness of the larger political system is reduced.

An ideal attainment of representativeness also carries with it the achievement of popular confidence that the country will be served by individuals of appropriate experience, ability, integrity, and by those given to sound policy, whichever side wins. An individual or group will prefer a party A over parties B and C, but if the nominees of the latter are perceived as incompetent or dangerous the democratic power struggle becomes overcharged.

Such a situation, in which the contrasting policy preferences of large groups of voters are reflected faithfully in the narrow field of candidates, while the ultimate victory of one contender is not seen by those who back the losers to carry prohibitively high costs, can never be easily achieved. In some democracies, indeed, it is perhaps not possible to achieve it at all, for divisions are too many and too deep—but this is only to restate the difficult, problematic character of representativeness.

An Organizing System. Parties are asked to arrange for effective competition and representation in the democratic struggle for elective office. Broadly important as these tasks are, they may in one sense be viewed as but focused applications of a single fundamental responsibility—that of organizing the polity for popular control.

A number of political commentators emphasize the primary importance of the organizing role of political parties. One component of the literature to which this group has contributed often is identified in terms of "the doctrine of responsible party government."* Austin Ranney has thus effectively summed up its perspective:

> There must exist at least two (and preferably only two) unified, disciplined political parties. Each has its conception of what the people want and a program of various measures designed to satisfy those wants. In a pre-election campaign each attempts to convince a majority of the people that its program will best do what the people want done. In the election each voter votes for a particular candidate in his district, primarily because that candidate is a member of the party which the voter wants to take power, and only secondarily because he prefers the individual qualities of one candidate to those of the other. The party which secures a majority of the offices of government in the election then takes over the entire power of the government and the entire responsibility for what the government does. It then proceeds to put its program into effect. . . . At the next election

---

* Among the more important works in this area are Woodrow Wilson's *Congressional Government* (Boston: Houghton Mifflin, 1885); E. E. Schattschneider's *Party Government* (New York: Farrar and Rinehart, 1942); and Austin Ranney's excellent review of the history and focus of the argument, *The Doctrine of Responsible Party Government* (Urbana: University of Illinois Press, 1962). A report made in 1950 by the Committee on Political Parties of the American Political Science Association (chaired by Schattschneider)—"Toward a More Responsible Two-Party System," *American Political Science Review*, supplement (September 1950)—articulated many of the perspectives in this literature.

the people decide whether, on the whole, they approve of the general direction that the party in power has been taking.*

This full "party government" position continues to strike one as unfortunate because it asks too much—and in so doing manages to convince many observers of its impracticality. It sets an extreme as the ideal. It calls for a type of centralized control in the party system which is quite unattainable, given the diversity of American society and the decentralization inherent in a constitutional system created to disperse power. It may even posit a centralization which is undesirable when set against the requirements of pluralism. Still, the basic concept which underlies the party government position seems sound. Only parties can so organize the issues that mass publics are enabled to speak effectively upon them. When they provide the "conduit or sluice by which the waters of social thought and discussion are brought to the wheels of political machinery and set to turn those wheels,"† parties energize public opinion and extend institutional responsiveness. If they make elected officials in some sense collectively—rather than individually—responsible to the electorate, parties enormously expand the level of meaningful public control over government.

The Present Status of the American Parties

The arguments of the three chapters that follow touch upon a number of issues, but they are directed primarily to the present inability of the U.S. party system to sufficiently organize, represent, and compete. Chapter 1 examines the de-

---

* Ranney, *op. cit.*, p. 12.
† The quotation is from Ernest Barker, *Reflections on Government* (London: Oxford University Press, 1942), p. 39.

terioration of the Republicans into "half a party," into permanent and increasingly ineffectual minority status. No major
party has been so weakly situated vis-à-vis its principal rival as
is the GOP today since the death-throes of the Federalists in
the second decade of the last century. This diminished standing involves more than the fact that the Republicans now cannot even hope to win control in such arenas as Congress and
most state legislatures. The GOP has as well experienced such
losses among critical elites that it no longer appears as a cred-
ible governing party. It is seen by much of informed opinion in
the country as a parochial and reactive alliance, increasingly
so, and this alienation of informed opinion constitutes an almost insuperable barrier to the development of an effective
alternate public philosophy.

The Republicans are not, of course, the only—nor even the
chief—losers in the saga of party decline that Chapter 1 re-
lates. With its "one-and-a-half-party system," the U.S. polity
manifests a decided loss of capacity for popular control.

Underchallenged by their opposition, and recognized as
both the pioneers and the continuing champions of the New
Deal "service state"—so staunchly supported by most of the
populace—the Democrats have reaped handsome electoral re-
wards. But as Chapter 2 points out, the Democratic coalition
has become so large and disparate that it cannot hold together
under any real pressure—the sort that gets applied in the
quadrennial presidential sweepstakes. It contains within itself
many of the fundamental divisions of the society, conflicts that
should be regularly pursued and made intelligible by interparty competition rather than confused by sporadic intraparty
feuding.

Both the Democrats and the Republicans confront serious
problems in representing the preferences of their ranks and
file, especially in the selection of presidential nominees. Over
the past four presidential elections, we have seen a series of

successful and near-successful candidacies of a very distinctive ideological character: Goldwater in 1964, McCarthy in 1968, McGovern in 1972, and Reagan in 1976. In each case the contender was the first choice of only a distinct minority of all adherents of the party and as well enjoyed the support of just a small fraction of the regular party leadership. Yet two of these unrepresentative candidates managed to capture their parties' nominations, and the other two came very close indeed.

Why the parties find their capacity to produce representative nominees diminished is explored in the chapters which follow. The precipitants of this change are both exogenous to the party system, involving especially the ideological orientations of groups of political activists, and products of internal alterations which have been imposed on party nomination machinery in the name of reform.

A substantial price has been paid for the breakdown in party representativeness. In 1972, for example, Richard Nixon won an overwhelming three-to-two victory over George McGovern, not because the voters wished to confer so decisive a blessing upon the administration's policies or upon the personal leadership style of the president, but simply because Senator McGovern was not acceptable to—was not seen as properly representing—a very substantial segment of his party's regular supporters. Many voters in an instance like this feel deprived of a satisfactory choice. A big majority is produced, but it is in no sense a mandate. The failure of representation leads to a lack of competitiveness and a general atmosphere of negativism—reducing the incentive to participate and rendering the campaign a far less meaningful medium for policy debate. A demoralized opposition is unable to test the victors effectively. Rank-and-file voters come to question the responsiveness of the parties to popular interests and expectations.

Overall, as Chapter 3 argues, the American political parties now manifest a diminished institutional presence. As labels, as names on the ballot, they are alive and well, but as organizations they have withered. Thus, the parties are less able than at any time since they attained mature form early in the nineteenth century to plan for and to arrange nominee selection. While their capacity to organize the government has never been what the "responsible party government" advocates have wanted, what little mortar parties once provided is now crumbling. Party is less relevant to the governing process in the U.S. today than ever before; as a result, government has lost an instrument for harnessing together its diverse and centrifugally inclined parts.

Now in the 1970s, the U.S. party system presents us with a case of institutional failure. In the pages that follow I try to describe this development, to explore its causes, to examine some of its consequences. The problem is substantial—I will resist the temptation to call it a "crisis"—and one not easily corrected. There is the need to rebuild the institutional parties on behalf of popular responsiveness and control. This can be done. But I see few signs now of an ability or inclination to do so.

WHERE HAVE ALL THE VOTERS GONE?

CHAPTER 1

☆ ☆ ☆ ☆ ☆ ☆

The Unmaking
of the Republican Party

*F*EW INSTITUTIONS IN THE U.S. HAVE BEEN SUBJECT TO MORE wildly fluctuating assessments over the last quarter-century than the Republican party. Seen destined to wander forever in the political wilderness following its fifth straight presidential defeat in 1948, the GOP was widely viewed in the five years or so surrounding the Eisenhower victories of the 1950s as riding a wave of national affluence and "middle classness" back to majority party status. But then came the Goldwater debacle of 1964 and, with it, renewed prophecies of Republican electoral doom. Just a half-decade later, however, with Richard M. Nixon occupying the White House and the Democrats in disarray, visions of "an emerging Republican majority" again began dancing—and not just in the head of Kevin P. Phillips, the young Republican strategist whose book gave wide frequency to the phrase.* Watergate, the forced resignation of a Republican president and a vice-president, and the GOP losses of 1974 and 1976 have now vanquished the party's hopes of a few years past, and once again questions of the continued electoral viability of the (once) Grand Old

---

* Kevin P. Phillips, *The Emerging Republican Majority* (New Rochelle, N.Y.: Arlington House, 1969).

Party are being raised—even by its own leaders. "I think a lot of us, including me, who have indulged in the rhetoric that the party can come back haven't really believed it ourselves," says Senator Paul Laxalt of Nevada, who was Ronald Reagan's campaign chairman in 1976.*

This roller-coaster treatment of Republican fortunes has not been very enlightening. When the party is first granted incipient majority status and then consigned to an early death every eight years, the predictions lose any claim to be taken seriously. They amount to episodes in a long-running soap opera, "The Perils of the GOP." Will the Republican party go the way of the Federalists and the Whigs? Or will it capture "the new majority"? Tune in again next election year.

Yet behind the melodrama, some real and consequential changes have been occurring in the condition of the Republican party. The GOP may have had "good years" in 1956, 1968, and 1972, and "bad years" in 1958, 1964, and 1974—but ups and downs in individual elections are inevitable. The important question is: Which way are things trending? For the Republicans during this past decade and a half, they have been trending downward—so steeply, in fact, that by now the trend has begun to reshape U.S. political life as a whole.

From a Decline to a Disaster

The GOP's fall from grace during the Depression decade has been amply chronicled. Less often noted is the overall strength that the party showed after the initial outpouring of economic distress–based protest had waned and the Democrats as incumbents encountered problems of their own. By 1940, for example, the Republicans trailed the Democrats in party iden-

---

* Interview with Senator Laxalt, May 10, 1977.

tification by only 6 percent, 43 to 37, with 20 percent of the public "independents," according to Gallup surveys. A decade and a half later, the Democrats' "identification edge" over the Republicans was at this same—significant but rather modest— level. It took the GOP but a decade after their 1932 rout to return to a strongly competitive position in Congress and the state legislatures. Of the 430 representatives elected to Congress in 1942, 208 bore the Republican label. The party captured both the House and Senate in 1946, repeated this in 1952, and otherwise stayed close to the Democrats throughout the 1950s until the 1958 recession-year election. As early as 1938 the Republicans had climbed back to a respectable 43 percent of state legislators nationwide—and a clear majority outside the South. In 1948 the GOP actually gained a state legislative edge by a margin of 53 to 47 percent, though the Democrats retained the presidency and regained a congressional majority. By all measures, the GOP in the 1940s and 1950s was the second party, but one able to seize power at all levels of government at any time.

The Republican erosion of the 1960s and 1970s is perhaps more consequential, *from the standpoint of the operations of the party system,* than the party's earlier Depression-bred plunge. For everywhere outside contests for the presidency and a handful of other highly visible offices which have become, increasingly, media-bounded responses to individual candidates, and not partisan affairs, the GOP no longer can provide reasonably close, sustained competition.

The 1976 contest between Jerry Ford and Jimmy Carter was very, very close. The results of the *overall* competition between the Democratic and Republican parties, though, proved exceptionally one-sided, as the "electoral box score" in Table 1, computed after the 1976 elections, indicates.

The Republican party now lacks any "turf" that is securely its own. Its overall electoral strength, as expressed, for example,

TABLE 1.
How the Two Parties Stood after the 1976 Election

	Republican	Democratic	Independent Other
Party Identification (Gallup)	22%	47%	31%
Members of Congress:	181	354	—
House	143	292	—
Senate	38	62	—
Proportion of the House of Representatives, popular vote nationally:	42	56	2
in the East	41	57	2
in the South	37	62	2
in the Midwest	47	52	1
in the West	43	55	2
Governors	12	37	1
National Conference of State Legislators: Members of state legislatures	2370	5128	55*
Proportions of state legislators	31	68	1
State house control by party nationally:	18	80	1*
in the East	5	13	—
in the South	0	32	—
in the Midwest	5	17	1*
in the West	8	18	—
States with both houses of the legislature and the governor of the same party	1	29	—

* The unicameral Nebraska legislature in fact controlled by the Republicans is technically nonpartisan.

in congressional balloting, has been eroding in many once-secure areas. At the same time, as congressional vote Maps 1 and 2 document, the GOP has been gaining ground—in some cases, quite dramatically—all across the South Atlantic and South Central states. There are 1,148 counties in the eleven states of the Old Confederacy; and in 1,001 of them the average Republican share of the two-party congressional vote was *higher* in the six elections from 1964 through 1974 than in the six elections of 1952–1962—even though the party's position elsewhere in the country *deteriorated*. The median percentage point gain for the Republicans in all 1,148 southern counties was 11.4, from 1952–1962 to 1964–1974.

This Republican congressional vote surge in Dixie is impressive, but so far it has fallen short of its mark—making the party an effective challenger to the Democrats. Only at the presidential vote level is the long-predicted "two-party South" a reality.

Outside the South, the Republicans have lost an enormous amount of ground over the last decade and a half. In the Northeast, for example, they were the majority party as recently as 1956, when they won 55.1 percent of the two-party congressional vote. In 1976 they trailed the Democrats by 16 percentage points in the New England and Middle Atlantic states.

A Cipher among Blacks

Thus the Republicans are now an exceptionally weak second party nationwide—weaker, for instance, than the Democrats were around 1900. They can win some elections, but they cannot win most of them and so cannot govern. For a quarter-century, the Democrats have held a majority in both houses of

The Decline of a Political Party

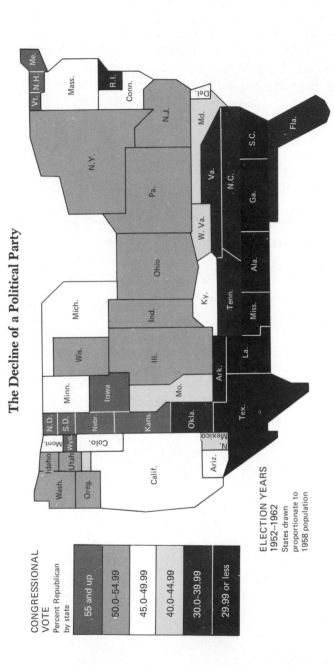

ELECTION YEARS
1952–1962
States drawn
proportionate to
1958 population

CONGRESSIONAL
VOTE
Percent Republican
by state

| 55 and up |
| 50.0–54.99 |
| 45.0–49.99 |
| 40.0–44.99 |
| 30.0–39.99 |
| 29.99 or less |

The best measure of a political party's underlying strength is the vote won by its legislative candidates over several elections. These maps show the average vote, by state, for Republican candidates for the U.S. House of Representatives during two periods—1952–1962 and 1964–1974. Two basic trends stand out. First, since the 1950s the Republicans have lost majority status in all but a handful of states, most of them small ones. Sec-

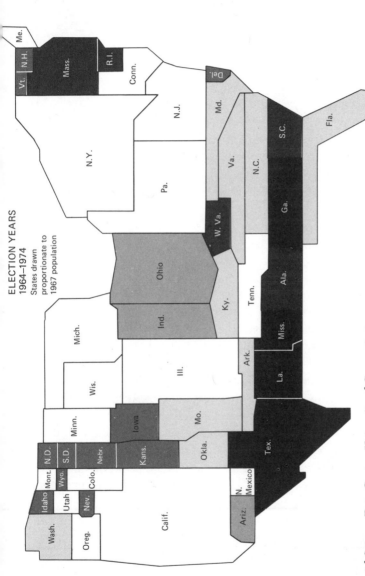

ELECTION YEARS
1964–1974
States drawn
proportionate to
1967 population

SOURCE: Social Science Data Center, University of Connecticut.

ond, the partisan attachments of the U.S. electorate as a whole have become more homogeneous geographically, as Republican strength has risen in the South and declined elsewhere. The size of the states in these maps reflects their share of U.S. population.

Congress, and Republican leaders no longer even suggest that their party might turn the tables.

What accounts for the GOP's decline during the past decade and a half? The 1976 presidential election highlighted one important factor—the party's failure to win support outside a narrow slice of the social spectrum, and especially its failure in the black community. Jimmy Carter won the backing of about 90 percent of the 5.8 million black Americans who went to the polls in 1976, giving him a margin of more than 4.7 million votes over Ford within the black community alone. Considering that Carter's national margin was only 1.7 million, and that many of his state pluralities were small, the Republicans' extreme weakness among blacks was not without significance for the outcome of the election.

An Act of Supreme Stupidity

Though we tend to forget it, the GOP's cipher status among blacks is a recent thing. Richard Nixon, for instance, received the support of only one black voter in eight in his 1972 landslide victory, but he was backed by almost *one-third* of black Americans in his narrow 1960 defeat. The Democrats now lead the party of Lincoln in partisan identification among blacks by an extraordinary 74-percentage-point margin, 79 to 5. In 1960 the Democratic lead was a far more modest 36 points, 58 to 22.

The key event in this shift of black allegiances was the 1964 election. Until that year, it was a question as to which of the two parties would be the party of civil rights. Outside the South, the Democrats were the more committed, but the GOP was not burdened with a large anti–civil rights southern wing. In an act of supreme stupidity, the GOP squandered that advantage when the Goldwater Republicans seized the cloak of racial resistance that the Democrats, by themselves, had been unable to shed. Ever since, the Democrats have been *the* party of civil rights. The narrow base of the GOP is also reflected in its poor showing among some other important groups. Catholics and Jews are grossly underrepresented in its ranks. To a striking extent, the Republicans have become a party of northern white Protestants. In 1976, for example, 56 percent of all those identifying themselves as Republicans were northern white Protestants, compared to 25 percent of Democrats. This WASPish image, and the reality it reflects, has seriously weakened the Republicans' ability to recruit in an ethnically diverse society.

TABLE 2.
The Ethnic Distribution of Republican and Democratic Identifiers, 1976.

	Democrats	*Republicans*
White Protestants	71	43
Northern	56	25
Southern	15	18
White Catholics	20	30
Blacks	3	18
Jews	1	3
Others	5	6

SOURCE: These data are from fifteen national surveys conducted in 1976 by the Gallup Organization. The total number of cases for this combined data set is 23,086.

But the real news about the Republican party isn't to be found in statistics about its imbalanced racial-ethnic makeup. Catholic Americans of most ethnic backgrounds, for example, have been disproportionately Democratic for over a century, and the falling away of black support from the GOP began nearly half a century ago. What *is* news—and what suggests the depth of the Republicans' problems these days—is that the GOP, a coalition once virtually synonymous with the middle class, now commands the allegiance of a distinct minority of middle-class Americans.

The idea that there is an inherent affinity between the middle classes and the Republican party has not died easily; over the years, it has undergone an interesting transformation while trying to catch up with a disappearing reality. At its birth, the GOP was the party of industrial development, and its aspirations were indeed intertwined with those of the entrepreneurial middle class.

The first big mistake of those who believed in the "middle-class-loves-the-Republicans" myth came in assuming that the pre-Depression middle class would be duplicated by the vastly larger middle class that developed after World War II. Not until 1951 was the mistake uncovered, when Samuel Lubell pointed out that "in large part, as the poor and underprivileged prospered and climbed they remained loyal to the Democratic party. The new middle class . . . seems as Democratic by custom as the older middle class elements are instinctively Republican."*

Myth No. 2 Bites the Dust

Version 1 of the "middle-class-loves-the-Republicans" argument thus expired. But a second version continued to enjoy a lively existence. It held that the Republicans are the party of the privileged strata. If the expanded middle class as a whole was no longer Republican, the reasoning went, then surely the upper middle class would remain tied to the party. And, indeed, this relationship did hold for a long time. Through the 1950s, a large majority of professionals, executives, managers, and the college-educated displayed Republican preferences.

---

* Samuel Lubell, *The Future of American Politics* (Garden City, N.Y.: Doubleday Anchor Books, revised edition, 1956), p. 62.

But sometime during the late 1950s and early 1960s, as Figures 1 and 2 show, there was a pronounced move toward the Democrats within the upper middle class. In 1964, for the first time, Democrats outnumbered Republicans throughout most of this stratum, in terms of both self-identification and voting. While there was some temporary falling off of Democratic support immediately after 1964, the overall trend has not been interrupted in the years since, and today a majority of the "privileged" are Democrats.

Nowhere is the Republican middle-class decline more evident than among those new entrants to middle-class occupations, the college students. The Republicans' share of student support reached its all-time low in 1974—just 14 percent as against 37 percent Democratic and 49 percent independent—and has not risen significantly since. Among students enrolled in graduate schools, an unbelievably low proportion of 9 percent identified with the GOP. And among students at major colleges and universities—those most likely to be members of the future elite—Republican electoral support falls *below* that within the general student population. Thus, in the spring of 1974, only 9 percent of Harvard undergraduates were registered as Republicans, whereas 57 percent were Democrats.

As these facts came to be recognized, people shifted to Version 3 of the "Republican–middle-class" myth—that a new petite bourgeoisie, angered by the special privileges won by the upper classes and given to the lower classes, is the GOP's last best hope. According to this notion, the Republicans' natural support comes from hard-working, law-abiding, middle-income whites, and especially from white Protestants in the South and white Catholics in the North. Kevin Phillips was one of the first to articulate this theory, and by now many Republicans accept it. "I think our constituency lies in the people paying the taxes," says Paul Laxalt. "The people at the top of the scale aren't worth a damn. Right below that are millions of

FIGURES 1 AND 2.

The Decline of the Republican Middle-Class Support: Party Identification and Congressional Vote, 1940–1976

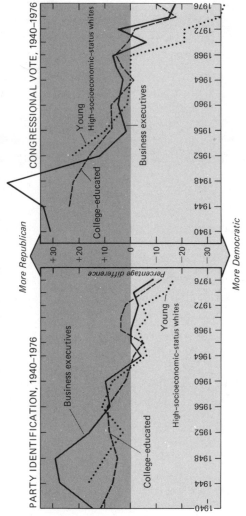

SOURCE: These distributions are based on Gallup survey data, made available by the Gallup Organization through the Roper Center.

people—small shop owners, what little is left of private enterprise—who pay their taxes. And down below you have beneficiaries of the system. Our constituency lies squarely in the
middle."*

The protesting lower middle class may well be the natural
constituency of the GOP—but if so, these voters don't know it
yet. Today the constitutents Phillips saw as building blocks of a
new Republican majority remain solidly Democratic. There
have been instances, to be sure, when middle-class protest has
materialized under the Republican banner, notably in the 1972
presidential contest. But there has been no consistent movement toward the GOP on the part of these groups. Today, the
Republicans enlist the support of only 18 percent of the middle-
income skilled workers, 16 percent of middle-income Catholics,
and 19 percent of middle-income white southerners. Two to
three times as many members of these groups describe themselves as Democrats.

The Establishment Party Loses the Establishment

Probably no notion is more deeply embedded in the conven-
tional American political wisdom than the belief that the
Republicans are the party of the old establishment—of Wall
Street and the eastern banking interests, of big business generally, of graduates of the elite ivy universities. And, indeed,
before and during the New Deal years, it was the case that the
Republicans were such an establishment party.

Today all this has changed. The change is rooted in the fact
that in a "postindustrial" era, new centers of power have developed. Rising affluence, advancing technology, the growing
importance of knowledge and communications, and the in-

---

* Interview with Senator Laxalt, May 10, 1977.

creasing resort to higher education have caused the intelligentsia—those trained in the use of ideas and involved in the culture—to attain unprecedented numbers and influence. For example, in 1940 there were 854,000 miners in the U.S. and 111,000 college professors. By 1970, the numbers of miners had shrunk to 164,000 while the population of college and university teachers had grown to 551,000.

As higher education became a leading postindustrial institution, so did local, state, and national government. In 1940 government at all levels employed 4.2 million people at a cost of a bit more than $20 billion. By 1976 it employed 15 million and spent around $575 billion. This expansion has been accompanied by a major increase in the power of governmental bureaucracies and of the people who run them.

There still is an establishment—comprising those with disproportionate influence in, if not control over, major institutions. But its composition has been changed mightily.

"Us" Versus "Them"

The emergence of these new elite groups was naturally accompanied by a shift of elite loyalties away from the Republicans. One would hardly expect the leadership of the U.S. higher-education establishment, for example, to support the Republicans, the party more strongly inclined to resist educational expenditures.

The extent to which the U.S. establishment is no longer primarily a big business establishment became apparent, particularly to Republicans, during the 1960s. In that decade, for the first time, GOP spokesmen started to sound like no one so much as the antiestablishment Bryan Democrats of seventy years earlier, as, for example, in the Nixon administration's occasional attacks on the news media. In *Before the Fall*, William Safire has described the "us against them" mentality in the inner circles of the administration he served—"them," in this case, being elitism generally, "social planners," the eastern establishment, the Washington establishment, the Kennedy apparat, and the establishment media.*

Today, we are seeing acted out the final chapter of the fall of the GOP from establishment status. Not only are new elite groups looking to the Democrats, but important segments of the old, once solidly Republican elites are now falling away from the GOP. Notable here is the deterioration of Republican support within the leadership of major business corporations. This shift will not be completed overnight, since a lot of historic attachments and some persisting elements of mutual self-interest remain. But signs of defection by big business are already evident.

One of the rudest shocks to confront Republicans as they surveyed the results of the 1976 election involved the flow of business money. The Federal Election Campaign Act of 1971 and its subsequent amendments allowed business firms to spend corporate funds on the administration of political action committees (PACs) for collecting and disseminating funds in federal campaigns. Many Republican leaders had expected PACs to be a useful, aboveboard means of bringing additional business contributions to GOP congressional candidates.

It has not worked out that way. While organized labor was distributing 97 percent of its congressional campaign contributions to Democrats in 1976, the business and trade-association PACs divided their contributions rather evenly—57 percent for the Republicans, 43 percent for Democratic candidates. Recognizing the fact of a permanent Democratic majority in

---

* William Safire, *Before the Fall: An Inside View of the Pre-Watergate White House* (Garden City, N.Y.: Doubleday, 1975), pp. 307–15.

Congress, business does appear to steer its contributions, as GOP chairman William Brock charges, "to buy access to Congress."*

"People Like That Don't Deserve to Survive"

This infuriates conservative Republicans, who more and more want, in the words of one of them, to "get the *Fortune* 500 off our backs." For unlike a lot of executives, the conservatives still believe, at least most of the time, in limited government, separation of the public and private sectors, and an arm's-length relationship between business and the state. "Big business is too often looking for special economic favors," argues Oklahoma Congressman Mickey Edwards, who is heralded in conservative circles as a rising star. "The Republican party ought to sever its ties to big business and support the free-enterprise system."†

Edwards's views are typical of many conservatives, who see corporate executives as apolitical, lacking in firm beliefs, and quite happy to comply with whatever the government wants, so long as they can maintain their stations in life and turn a profit. "People like that," Congressman Edwards says bitterly, "don't deserve to survive."‡

The View from the Fortieth Floor

For their part, many business leaders are more than a little impatient with the GOP. To them, the moderates in the party,

---

* William Brock, "The GOP and the Fortune 500," *Wall Street Journal*, March 23, 1977.
† Interview with Congressman Mickey Edwards, May 9, 1977.
‡ *Ibid.*

though ideologically acceptable, haven't shown the ability to keep themselves in power or manage the country's affairs, while the conservative wing seems unable to come to grips with the complexities of the modern economy. One increasingly hears views like those of Augustine R. Marusi, chairman of Borden, Inc. "Theoretically, you'd think the Democratic party would tend to be more inflationary," he says. "But the fact is it was in Nixon's administration that we got the big inflation. I think that the Carter administration could very well do a much better job on inflation."*

To be sure, most corporate executives still identify with the GOP. In a 1976 *Fortune* survey, 56 percent of the chief executive officers of the *Fortune* 500 called themselves Republicans, 6 percent Democrats, and 37 percent said they were independents.† But these loyalties lack passion. Top executives may still be Republican, but they are no longer *partisan*. Professional managers who deal with the big world, most of them have come to think it does not usually make all that much difference which party wins, and indeed that business and the country often fare better under the Democrats. Observes Rawleigh Warner, Jr., the chairman of Mobil: "I would have to say that in the last ten to fifteen years, business has fared equally well, if not better, under Democratic administrations as under Republican administrations."‡ Other top executives echo Warner's sentiments.

Thus big business, once a source of bitter opposition to the New Deal, has made peace with it. Like big education, big labor, and big science, big business is a claimant and a beneficiary of the governmental order Franklin D. Roosevelt began to assemble. The fact that the GOP is on the verge of seeing its

---

* Interview with Augustine R. Marusi, June 9, 1977.
† Charles G. Burck, "A Group Profile of the Fortune 500 Chief Executive," *Fortune*, vol. 93, no. 5 (May 1976), p. 177.
‡ Interview with Rawleigh Warner, Jr., June 10, 1977.

special relationship with corporate business come to an end is a telling indication of how much the party has ceased to be an instrument of elites and become instead a vehicle of neopopulist reaction.

The pronounced weakening of the Republican base among those who lead the major corporations does not mean, of course, that the party is finding itself without significant backing within the business community generally. Small entrepreneurial business remains soldily Republican. And newer large-scale industries, located disproportionately in the South and West, firms often headed by "old-style" entrepreneurial types rather than by salaried managers, continue to favor decidedly conservative policies—and to contribute heavily to the conservative wing of the GOP. Thornton Bradshaw of Atlantic Richfield commented on this sharp division in outlook organized on a managers-entrepreneurs axis. To the extent that the "Reagan wing gains ascendancy in the Republican party nationally, support for the party will drop further among the professional management of the larger corporations. In terms of the individual entrepreneurs who are ever hopeful of the day when the tax situation will be changed so that they too can build up a large fortune, however, the GOP's position will not be weakened.*

A Coalition or a Church?

Over the last fifteen years, the center of gravity in the Republican party has moved rightward. In part, the shift reflects the development of a serious Republican organization in the South. Once upon a time, the Republican party in most of

---

* Interview with Thornton Bradshaw, June 7, 1977.

Dixie was a "patronage party," whose leaders, having no prospect of winning locally, were largely concerned with capturing the White House and the patronage it could hand out. Now they want national nominees who can help them with the local electorate, and they have concluded that conservative candidates best fill the bill. Thus, for the foreseeable future, moderate to liberal Republicans will never again enjoy the kind of support among southern delegates that Dwight Eisenhower had in his contest with Robert A. Taft.

The South aside, the GOP has been losing adherents since 1960, and these losses have been concentrated among liberal and moderate elements. As a result, the party has become more conservative and has found it harder to generate a broad appeal. Walter Dean Burnham, a political scientist at the Massachusetts Institute of Technology, summarizes the point this way: "The smaller a minority becomes, the more likely it is that its extreme tendencies will become overrepresented . . . and then gain more control over the party . . . which causes the party to continue to lose ground."*

The GOP's movement to the right has transformed intraparty conflict. Until about a decade ago, the main Republican division was between a conservative wing and a moderate-liberal faction. This description no longer holds. The old moderate-liberal leaders have not disappeared, to be sure—the Cases, Javitses, and Percys are still around—but they can no longer seriously contest for control of the national party. The really consequential split within the GOP today is between two conservative wings that are divided, not over ideology, but over the question of what a party is and what course the GOP should

---

* Interview with Walter Dean Burnham, conducted by Jim Bell of the Boston Bureau of *Time* magazine, June 1, 1977. The author wishes to express his appreciation to the editors of Time Inc., for making available the text of this and other interviews conducted by the *Time* staff.

chart in the context of American politics. The struggle is an important one, and the way it is resolved could decide the party's very survival.

The question is: Is the Republican party a "church" or a "coalition"? One group wants the Republicans to be an ideological church—an institution for conservative believers. The metaphor should not be overdrawn; few are prepared to argue that anyone not subscribing to a tightly defined credo should be excommunicated. But one group of GOP leaders, associated disproportionately with the Reagan candidacy, do feel, as did their counterparts in the Goldwater movement, that there is a conservative majority out there waiting to be mobilized by dedicated conservative leadership. The Republican party, according to this view, needs to be more principled and to offer "a choice, not an echo."

Although the Reaganites are the church faction, the principal leaders of the Reagan presidential bid—campaign chairman Paul Laxalt and campaign manager John Sears—are strong critics of the church approach. Their decision to name Senator Richard Schweiker, a liberal, as Reagan's running mate reflected their belief, shared by many in the party, that the GOP is a coalition. The "coalitionists" see the party as a diverse assortment of people and interests and are persuaded that compromise is part of the necessary stuff of politics, that one can win only with diversity in the American two-party system. Gerald Ford, a committed coalitionist, is even more frustrated by the "church mentality" than are many of his liberal colleagues. Speaking at a Republican dinner in New York on June 16, 1977, Ford exclaimed: "I am sick and tired of those who want to prove they are purer of philosophy. Fling those doors open."

One important area where this division between the "church" and "coalition" factions in the GOP comes to the surface involves the issue of whether the party should make a strong appeal to black voters. In urging such an effort, Republican national chairman William Brock has asserted repeatedly that "we're determined again to become the party of Lincoln and freedom." The conservative leader of the Republican House minority, John Rhodes of Arizona, has been even more emphatic: "It's hard to pinpoint precisely when it happened . . . when the party of Abraham Lincoln forgot its heritage and started neglecting minorities. But somewhere along the way the Republican party became exclusionary. . . . Today's Republican leadership is trying hard to change all this. We are engaged in a serious effort to convince black Americans that they can have a home in our party and that we want them to have a home in our party."*

Other Republican conservatives, of course, take issue with the Brock-Rhodes stance. Writing in the *New York Times*, Patrick Buchanan belittled a "rattled Republican chairman," i.e., William Brock, for his decision to "hurriedly set aside $750,000 for black Republican missionaries to carry the gospel to the inner city." It is simply a fact, Buchanan concludes, that the legitimate self-interests of the black community and of the Republican party clash. "The Republican philosophy of limited government is seen as colliding head-on with black America's perceived interest in the expansion of Federal power." He wants the Republican party to "face facts," to write off the black vote because it is part of the Democrats' irreducible core, and to concentrate on the white petite bourgeoisie.†

This debate over the desirability of Republican party-broadening through sustained overtures to the black community will doubtless continue. Whatever the Republican leadership does, it will find it extremely difficult to resurrect the party in black

---

* John J. Rhodes, "The GOP and Black America," *Congress Today*, (May 1977), p. 2.
† Patrick J. Buchanan, "Blacks and Republicans," *New York Times*, April 5, 1977.

America because (*a*) Democratic ties have become natural, and (*b*) the GOP is almost totally without an "infrastructure" in black areas. Still, proponents of the Buchanan position should take note of the following possibility: that by being shut out in the black community, the GOP forfeits more than the 4.7-million-vote plurality Jimmy Carter won from blacks in 1976; that it exposes itself as a party at war with "progressive" opinion. White America wants to eradicate the bitter legacy of slavery and "Jim Crow" segregation. It is divided, often deeply, over the means and the precise end results, but the general goal is widely shared. The Buchanan position, despite protests to the contrary, comes perilously close to suggesting a fundamental indifference to the goal. The GOP will remain decidedly the minority party in black America. But it is more than a little consequential what kind of a minority it will prove to be.

In Search of a Public Philosophy

Republicans of all persuasions agree that their party has too negative an image, that it should set forth its own positive ideas more attractively, and that it should make a more effective connection between the feelings in its gut and the aspirations of the American people. Some, like Senator Bob Packwood of Oregon, have made ambitious efforts in this direction. Packwood's view is that Americans demand many social-welfare programs and that the Republicans should stop resisting and become aggressive advocates of an expansion of social services —but through the private rather than the public sector.* In many ways, the times seem propitious for quests like Packwood's. The reigning American "public philosophy" of the last

---

* U.S. Senator Robert W. Packwood, speech given to the Corchester Conference, Seaside, Oregon, March 5, 1977.

four decades—New Deal liberalism—is reeling under the most serious challenge in its history. Yet if the Democrats (and the country) are thereby in trouble, the Republicans are poorly equipped to chart a new course.

In the first place, coherent and energizing public philosophies—those which are "progressive" in the sense that they are able to move the country in a direction desired by much of the population—don't exactly grow on trees. Indeed, in the last century only two have attained this status, the industrial nation-building ethos of the post–Civil War Republicans and New Deal liberalism. The alienation of informed opinion and the intellectual community from the GOP means that the party lacks the sort of people whose contributions are crucial to the formulation of an alternative to the liberal orthodoxy.

Even if these problems could be overcome and the Republicans could create a winning policy approach, it is doubtful that the party could introduce the new programs. American political parties are laterally, not hierarchically, organized. Only rarely, at moments of extreme crisis, is there a chance for a gifted leader to set a party on a new course. Usually there are just too many leaders, too many activists, too many special-interest constituencies standing in the way of efforts at redirection. The Republican party may at some future point benefit from its own version of the Great Depression and FDR, but Republicans are not advised to hold their breaths.

Thus today the GOP is left to grapple with the classic problem of minority parties—the division between a "me-too" wing and a backward-looking ideological faction. The me-tooers can win elections when they bring forth an attractive candidate, but imitating the opposition isn't a promising way to build a permanent majority. On the other hand, the ideological purists, who do offer an alternative, tend to lose disastrously whenever the party nominates one of their own, because they are seen by the public as mounting an attack on progress itself. Americans believe that the future will be better than the past, and they will not support a party that seems to argue for going backward. The persisting optimism nurtured by the American experience has made the country profoundly hostile to parties of nostalgia.

Just over a decade ago, in assessing the condition of the GOP in the wake of the Goldwater candidacy, Nelson Polsby, a political scientist at the University of California at Berkeley, wrote that the efforts then being made to revive the party "may be insufficient to prevent an effective shift in this country to a one-and-one-half-party system . . ."* Polsby seemingly was the first to evoke the image of a party system substantially altered by the enfeeblement of one of its members, and in the intervening years his prophecy has been fulfilled. The GOP today is in a weaker position than any major party of the U.S. since the Civil War.

"It May Look Dead but You Can Never Kill It"

Having fallen to this sorry state, the GOP suffers from a dynamic described by the adage, "Nothing fails like failure." Seeing it as an apparently permanent minority, groups still naturally inclined to the GOP give their support to Democrats for "practical" reasons. Bright young lawyers interested in political careers look to an ascendant party rather than to one in decline. And a steady stream of the "plight-of-the-GOP" stories may themselves reinforce the trend. "The Republican party's main threat," argues GOP consultant J. Brian Smith, "is the constant prediction that it's going to die."

Yet for all its weakness, the GOP does not appear about to go

---

* Nelson Polsby, "Strategic Considerations," in Milton Cummings (ed.), *The National Election of 1964* (Washington, D.C.: The Brookings Institution, 1966), p. 107.

the way of the Federalists and the Whigs. "The Republican party is like a fungus," observes John Sears. "It may look dead but you can never kill it." In leadership base and mass support —some 34 million adult Americans identify themselves as Republicans—the GOP dwarfs any possible rival for second-party status. The electoral laws powerfully bolster the two established parties and retard the development of challengers. And there does not at present appear to be any hook on which to hang a new major party, the wishful grousing of some conservatives to the contrary notwithstanding. Other prophecies would be more colorful, but the prospect is that the U.S. will continue to limp along with the confusion and diminished competitiveness of its new one-and-one-half-party system.

CHAPTER 2

☆　☆　☆　☆　☆　☆

The Divided Democrats

*I*T IS AN ARTICLE OF FAITH THESE DAYS, AND NOT ONLY
among Republican conservatives, that the United States
has moved to the right. The same notion is accepted by
many Democrats—including pollster Patrick Caddell, the official reader of tea leaves for the Carter White House, who as-
sured his boss in a much-leaked memorandum written in December 1976 that conservatives "have become a larger and larger block of the electorate."* Doesn't Jimmy Carter's amazing
and graceful triumph over a host of better-known Democratic
liberals in the 1976 nomination struggle prove as much? Maybe.
A host of public-opinion surveys do indicate that twice as
many Americans call themselves "conservative" as call themselves "liberal."

It is also widely believed that much of the public is mad at
the federal government. Jimmy Carter ran against "Washington" in 1976 and won. Ronald Reagan sounded a similar theme
and very nearly kept an incumbent Republican president from
getting his party's nomination. Three-fifths of the populace
profess to believe that "quite a few of the people" who run the
national government are at least a little crooked. Three Ameri-

---

* Patrick H. Caddell, "Initial Working Paper on Political Strategy,"
December 10, 1976, p. 17.

cans in five maintain that the federal government "is pretty much run by a few big interests." And three-fourths of the public say that government "wastes *a lot* of the money we pay in taxes."

Unquestionably, some important changes have taken place in public opinion. The evidence does not indicate, however, a decisive swing away from liberalism and big government. The public mood is far more complex and ambivalent.

Even as the proportion of self-described conservatives in the U.S. has been surging upward, the Democrats—the party of big, liberal government—have been *extending* their domain. So many Americans now vote so often for their candidates that the Democrats have become the established governing party to a degree unequaled by any other alliance since the Jeffersonians. This Democratic ascendency testifies to the strength of the appeal of many of the programs and of the governmental approach with which the party is associated. But it has also resulted from the insufficiencies of the Republican challenge.

Despite all of this, the Democrats *do* have a problem. For a supermajority party, they have an extraordinarily hard time of it trying to capture the presidency.

These seeming contradictions—a "conservative" people voting massively for the liberal party, a majority party that doesn't dominate the nation's highest office—reflect the fact that there is not one liberalism in America these days, but two. The first of these liberalisms in terms of historical appearance —the liberalism that shaped the New Deal—has now become well-nigh consensual. But over the last two decades there has emerged a second kind of liberalism that deeply divides the populace and fractures it along new lines.

The Democrats, to their joy and sorrow, are the party of both liberalisms. They have reaped a rich electoral harvest from the older version and continuing vulnerability from the newer. When the former has been permitted to dominate, as in most contests for public office, it has helped the Democrats defeat their opponents and has contributed to their now over-whelming lead. But the deep conflict surrounding the latter kind of liberalism has sometimes intruded, especially in the highly visible and symbolic contests for the presidency—and where it has Democratic candidates for the office are, if any-thing, the underdogs. Thus the U.S. today operates with a curious two-tier electoral system, and the overall effect is to confuse and blur popular expectations as to policy.

The Democrats' Claim

The foundation of the two-tier system is the widespread acceptance among Americans of one key element of New Deal policy. Consider, for example, the issue of public spending for social services. People may complain today that taxes are too high, that bureaucrats intrude too much, that "the govern-ment" wastes money. But ask them what they want to do in each specific policy sector, and they reply, "Keep going."

A 1976 survey by Potomac Associates, a Washington-based research group, inquired of a national cross-section of Ameri-cans whether "the amount of our tax money now being spent" for various activities should be increased, reduced, kept at the present level, or ended. Respondents were first urged to "bear in mind that sooner or later all government spending has to be taken care of out of the taxes you and other Americans pay." Despite this caution, the investigators found that the public "favored at least some increase in spending on the fifteen pro-grams at the top of the list," programs that virtually covered the waterfront of governmental activity, from developing energy self-sufficiency to aiding the elderly.*

---

* Edwin L. Dale, Jr., Donald R. Lesh, and Lloyd A. Free, *Priorities in an Uncertain Economy: Inflation, Recession, and Government Spend-ing, a Policy Perspective* (Washington, D.C.: Potomac Associates, 1976), pp. 18–25.

The Potomac inquiry did find the populace becoming slightly less enthusiastic about big government programs; the one exception is defense, where support for more spending has risen sharply. The most striking feature of the Potomac data, however, is the range and extent of public backing for government intervention in almost every conceivable area. A number of other surveys made over the past five years have found the same thing.°

Equally impressive is the degree to which this support spreads out across the social spectrum. The proportion of people from families earning $25,000 a year and higher who think government should spend more to improve education is almost identical to that of persons with annual family incomes of $7,000 and under. College graduates and those with less than a high school education are about equally supportive of greater federal expenditures on health services. Professionals and managers on the one hand, and unskilled workers on the other, give equal backing to increased spending on urban problems.†

There simply is no base for an anti–New Deal party. Yet a stale, declining distrust of New Deal programs, left over from the 1930s, is the closest thing the GOP has to a public philosophy.

To be sure, the general public is far from ecstatic about the current state of the nation. Dissatisfaction with the perfor-

---

° See, for example, the General Social Surveys, 1972–1977, of the National Opinion Research Center.

† According to the composite file of NORC General Social Survey data (one national survey each year, 1972–1976, with a total number of cases of 7,590) 51 percent of the highest income group ($25,000 and up) want more government spending for education; the proportion within the lowest income group ($7,000 and under) is 48 percent. Sixty-seven percent of college graduates, as compared to only 62 percent of those with less than high school training, want increased governmental spending in the health services area. People employed in professional and managerial jobs, and unskilled workers, each showed 56 percent in favor of increased spending to solve problems of the big cities.

CHART 1.

Nearly Everyone Loves Big Government: Levels of Public Support for New Deal Spending

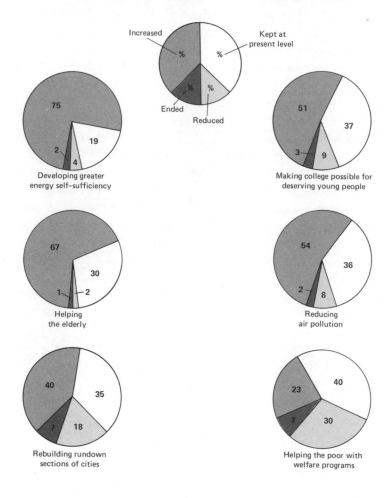

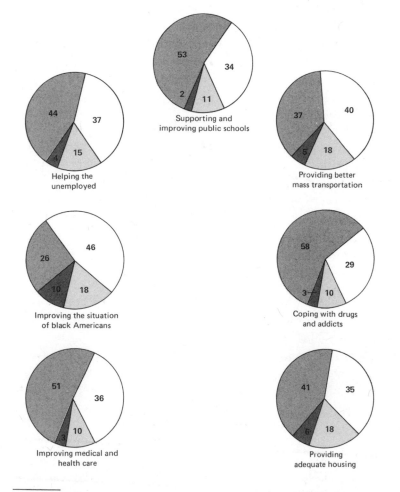

Helping the
unemployed

Supporting and
improving public schools

Providing better
mass transportation

Improving the situation
of black Americans

Coping with drugs
and addicts

Improving medical and
health care

Providing
adequate housing

SOURCE: These data are from a Spring 1976 survey conducted on behalf of Potomac Associates by the Gallup Organization. The data are reported in Dale, et al., *Priorities in an Uncertain Economy: Inflation, Recession, and Government Policy Perspective*, 1976.

mance of political leadership and government, as noted in the Introduction, has increased markedly over the past decade. But most of the discontent reflects a perceived lack of honesty and responsiveness on the part of politicians; it does not focus on any particular party. Where there has been some partisan "fallout," it is the GOP—in this post-Watergate period—that has suffered most.

The Everyone Party

As a result of public satisfaction with key elements of the New Deal state, and the failure of the party system generally to provide sustained contests for power around those issues and concerns which currently divide the populace, the Democrats have emerged almost everywhere outside the presidential arena as the "everyone party." The depiction is not intended literally, of course. Rather, it is meant to describe an essentially unprecedented situation in which one party shows more strength than its opposition across virtually the entire range of major social groupings. The Republicans do better among some groups than others, but almost no part of the populace regularly gives them pluralities.

The Democrats are, for example, well ahead of the GOP in every age group, from the youngest segment of the electorate to the oldest, and their margin is remarkably uniform. Wage workers are more Democratic than businessmen and executives, but a majority of even the latter now identify with the Democrats and vote for Democratic congressional candidates. All educational groups show a Democratic margin. So do all income levels, including the very prosperous. People who come from wealthy family backgrounds prefer the Democrats by a two-to-one margin. The Democrats lead the Republicans in

CHART 2.

The Surprising Politics of Self-Described Conservatives

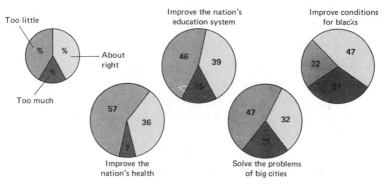

Are we spending too much, too little, or the right amount on programs to:

CONGRESSIONAL VOTE

PARTY IDENTIFICATION

SOURCE: The information on party identification and congressional support is from the composite 1976 Yankelovich data set. Conservative responses to questions of government spending are taken from the combined (1972–1976) NORC surveys.

every region, among all religious groupings, among virtually all ethnic groups.*

Perhaps the most striking of all, the Democrats lead not only among voters who think of themselves as liberals and moder-

---

* For a further elaboration of these data, see Ladd (with Charles D. Hadley), *Transformations of the American Party System* (New York: W. W. Norton, 1978, second edition), pp. 294–99.

ates, but even among self-described conservatives. A majority of such conservatives voted for Democratic congressional candidates in 1976, and more of them identify with the Democrats than with the GOP.*

But that isn't so surprising when you stop to consider that a majority of self-described conservatives—1970s style—strongly endorse New Deal spending programs. As Chart 2 indicates, overwhelming majorities of self-proclaimed conservatives want either to increase government spending in most of the principal policy areas, or at least to maintain existing programs. There may indeed be a conservative *majority* "out there," as the Republican right has insisted from Taft to Goldwater to Reagan, but it cannot be tapped by calls to cut back on federal expenditures.

"Some Democratic Era!"

So why have the Democrats had so much trouble with the presidency? The Republicans have won four of the eight post–World War II presidential elections. A Democratic presidential nominee has received an absolute majority of the popular vote only twice in the last eight contests, and only once has there been a decisive Democratic victory—Johnson's in 1964. Adding up all the presidential votes cast since World War II, the Republicans actually lead the Democrats, 271 million to 256 million. Contemplating such data, election analysts Richard Scammon and Ben Wattenberg exclaimed, "Some Democratic era!"

---

* According to Yankelovich survey data, 54 percent of self-described conservatives voted for Democratic congressional candidates in 1976, while only 46 percent of this ideological group supported Republicans. The seven 1976 Yankelovich surveys that were combined for purposes of analysis have a total *n* of 7,977.

But it is, of course, a Democratic era. The Democrats dominate the federal bureaucracy, Congress, the state legislatures, the governorships, and so forth. In 1972, when their presidential nominee was getting trounced by 18 million votes and giving birth to the adage, "as goes Massachusetts, so goes the District of Columbia," they were winning a majority of the popular vote in U.S. House of Representatives contests, a forty-six–seat edge in the House, and 60 percent of all state legislative seats. In 1976, while the Democrats barely managed a presidential victory, they won a 149-seat margin in the U.S. House, enjoyed a 14-percentage-point lead in the House popular vote, and dominated the state legislatures with 68 percent of all seats.

One reason for the sharp and persisting disparity between the Democrats' uncertain performance in presidential elections and their domination of everything else is that voting for the presidency has come to have less and less to do with the political party. The parties have been weakened organizationally in recent years, and the American electorate—better educated, more leisured, with more sources of political information, and hence more confident of its ability to judge candidates and programs without reference to their partisan origins—is less strongly attached to the parties and more inclined to vote independently than ever before.

Moreover, the emergence of television as the principal source of information about candidates for office—especially at the national levels, where media resources are so great—has transformed contests for the presidency (and a few other highly visible offices in large, media-rich states such as New York and California) into gigantic acts of theater. In the age of television, presidential contenders are brought instantaneously into voters' living rooms all across the nation. Does the candidate smile enough? Does he look nervous? Is too much perspiration collecting on his brow? Such considerations, together, to be sure, with what the candidate says, determine outcomes. Thus the presidency has been cut loose from the party. Contests for president surely manifest real competition—but it is a highly personalized type and thus changes massively from one election to the next.

Television not only cuts the presidency loose from party, it also intensifies that office's symbolic importance to the American people. The presidency has always combined head-of-government functions with the role of chief of state—the ceremonial representative of the United States. As Clinton Rossiter put it in his study of the office, "the President . . . is the one-man distillation of the American people just as surely as the Queen is of the British people; he is, in President Taft's words, 'the personal embodiment and representative of their dignity and majesty.'"*

Inevitably, then, in periods of change, as new issues rush across the national stage, it is the president more than any other public officeholder to whom the citizenry looks for cues and direction. There is intense concern among contending groups that this "bully pulpit" be used to advance their favored styles, programs, and values.

In contests for Congress and many lesser offices, by way of contrast, the individual candidates are much less visible. The controversial new issues are far more easily ducked, especially given what George Will has called "the poverty of Republican doctrine regarding the public's more central interests."† Democratic candidates have had little trouble "standing" on their support for more public service.

---

* Clinton Rossiter, *The American Presidency* (New York: New American Library, 1960, second edition), p. 16.
† The quotation is from the syndicated column of George F. Will, October 15, 1977.

The Ideology of the New Class

The heightened symbolic importance of the presidency has been a particular source for difficulty for the Democrats; for the last decade and a half in the U.S. has been a period of extraordinary social change and turbulence. During that time, it is true, the Old Liberalism that shaped the New Deal state was incorporated into the national consensus. But at the same time a New Liberalism began to emerge, and it has been giving Democratic candidates for the presidency fits.

The New Liberalism's attitudes are very different from— indeed, often at odds with—those of the New Deal liberals. For example, the New Liberals support the busing of school children to achieve racial integration; they reject "equality of opportunity," insisting instead upon "equality of result"; they want to extend civil liberties, notably the rights of the accused in criminal trials; and they sharply question the value of economic growth, believing that it damages the "quality of life." The New Liberalism also differs from the New Deal ethos in the matter of personal morality; it takes a libertarian stance on such issues as abortion, legalization of marijuana, homosexuality, and racial intermarriage.

The New Liberalism hardly generates consensus—either within the general public or among Democrats—for it is very much a class ideology. It comprises the political world view of what is now frequently dubbed the "New Class," a collectivity whose core appears to be college-educated professionals and managers in the public sector—in government and in educational, professional, and other social-service institutions. The New Class liberals are well placed and wield considerable influence within such major and expanding institutions as governmental bureaucracy, the press, the academy, and the culture generally. They are, however, a distinct minority in the nation as a whole—and their view is intensely controversial among the large traditional middle and working classes. The New Liberals can influence the choice of a presidential nominee and the shape of his campaign. But the candidate's appeal to the nation as a whole is thereby compromised.

The Bourgeois Workers

The New Liberalism is fraught with danger to a Democratic candidate today, in part because the vast majority of the population does not share its enthusiasm for social and cultural change. Much of the American working class has become bourgeois and is therefore anxious to protect a status gained at considerable effort and often tenuously held. Whereas policy innovation in the 1930s often involved efforts by the working class to strengthen its position vis-à-vis business, today the New Liberals' projects for social change impose some significant costs and risks on broad sectors of the working and middle classes, who do not hesitate to make their unhappiness known.

By contrast, the more affluent groups in a wealthy society like the U.S. today tend increasingly to assume outlooks that are independent of their relative economic standing. The upper middle class particularly, altered by the infusion of a large professional-managerial, public-sector cohort, has been detached from traditional business concerns. Its perspectives now seem to be shaped far more by universities and the intellectual community, and many of its members have come to share in some of the critical, change-demanding orientations that have long been associated with intellectual life.

The New Class and other upper strata also have a natural

concern about "life-styles" and cultural change—areas in which upper social groups have always been more receptive to change than the traditional middle and working classes. Cultural experimentation by upper social classes is not new. What is new is the size of this group in the U.S. today and the rapidity with which different value orientations are being introduced. Survey work by Daniel Yankelovich and his associates has shown that moral norms are changing extremely quickly in the higher-income groups these days. Their sexual attitudes are more liberal; their once automatic respect for established authority structures has declined; their embrace of "old-fashioned" patriotism has loosened; their orientations toward work, marriage, family, and the relative importance of material achievement have changed; and they manifest heightened concern with individual self-fulfillment and self-expression.*

Even Carter Got the Backlash

Thus the rise of the New Liberalism within the Democratic alliance creates a real problem for the party. The world views of New Class and Old Class Democrats are so sharply at odds that whenever a campaign serves to emphasize them, a serious rupture seems virtually inevitable. What is involved is nothing less than two world views, partly generational in origin, partly relating to different class experiences. To illustrate the extent of this divide, Table 1 shows the opinions on a range of these issues, of two groups of Democratic identifiers: persons under

---

* For further discussion of this ideological division involving the upper and middle-to-lower social strata, see Ladd, "Liberation Upside Down: The Inversion of the New Deal Order," *Political Science Quarterly* (Winter 1977), pp. 557–600; and *Transformations of the American Party System,* op. cit., especially chapters 4, 5, and 6.

TABLE 1.

"The War of the World Views": Attitudes of New Class and Old Class Democrats on Social and Cultural Issues

	New Class Democrats	Old Class Democrats
Should divorce be easier or more difficult to obtain than it is now?		
Percentage answering "easier"	59	21
Should a pregnant woman be able to obtain a legal abortion if she is married·an does not want any more children?		
Percentage answering "yes"	73	32
What is your opinion of someone having sexual relations with someone other than the marriage partner?		
Percentage thinking extramarital sex is always wrong	38	80
What is your opinion of sexual relations between two adults of the same sex?		
Percentage feeling homosexuality is always wrong	27	89
Do you think we are spending the right amount of money to protect the environment?		
Percentage thinking we are spending too little	85	49
Do you think there should be laws against marriages between blacks and whites?		
Percentage favoring laws against miscegenation	5	67

TABLE 1. (*cont'd*)

"The War of the World Views": Attitudes of New Class and Old Class Democrats on Social and Cultural Issues

	New Class Democrats	Old Class Democrats
Which statement comes closest to your feelings about pornography laws? Percentage thinking "there should be laws against the distribution of pornography *whatever the age*"	13	55
In a community-wide vote on the housing issue, which law would you favor? Percentage choosing law allowing homeowner to decide, even if he prefers not to sell to blacks	33	72

NOTE: New Class Democrats are respondents under forty years of age, college-educated, in professional and managerial jobs. Old Class Democrats are those over age fifty, without college training, in blue-collar occupations. The data are from the combined 1972–1976 NORC surveys.

forty years of age, who are college graduates and in professional and managerial jobs; and men and women fifty years and older, with high school educations or less, employed in blue-collar positions. Fifty-nine percent of the former group, believe divorces should be made easier to attain, the position of just 21 percent of the latter. Seventy-three percent of the high-status Democrats think women should be able to obtain abortions for no other reason than that they desire no more children, while only 32 percent of the lower-status partisans take this stand. Among the young, college-trained professionals and managers, just 38 percent maintain that extramarital sexual relations are always wrong, while 80 percent of the older blue-collar Democrats hold to this view. Just over a quarter (27 percent) of the former group reject homosexuality, the stance of 89 percent of the latter. Two-thirds of the young Democrats of high socioeconomic standing insist that an individual selling his home should be barred by law from refusing to sell it to a black, whereas just one-fifth (22 percent) of the older, lower-status Democrats support such legislation. And so it goes across the entire range of new social and cultural issues.

Over the past decade or so the tendency to call attention to this divide has been far greater at the presidential level than in other contests. The most dramatic instance, of course, was the 1972 presidential race, in which George McGovern took up the New Liberal banner, was thereby seen an unrepresentative nominee by large numbers of regular Democratic partisans, and was buried electorally by a flawed, unattractive, never especially popular Republican. But even Jimmy Carter in 1976 was not immune to anti–New Liberal backlash. Thus, while 54 percent of those describing themselves as "conservatives" voted Democratic in the 1976 congressional elections, only 37 percent of them backed Carter.

The two-tier electoral system is now in full swing, as Figures 1 and 2 testify. The two groups they depict–white southerners and big-city white Catholics in the North—have been important adherents of the New Deal Democratic coalition. In their party identification and congressional voting, they have remained securely in the Democratic camp over the last decade and a half. In presidential balloting, however, both of these pivotal groups have ceased being dependably Democratic.

Just how undependable they are was made clear in the 1976 election. Among white southerners, for example, Jimmy Carter, a native Georgian, did far better than George McGovern had four years earlier, as might be expected. The pull of south-

FIGURES 1 AND 2.

The Rise of the Two-Tier Electoral System: Party Preferences of White Southerners and Big-City Catholics, 1960–1976

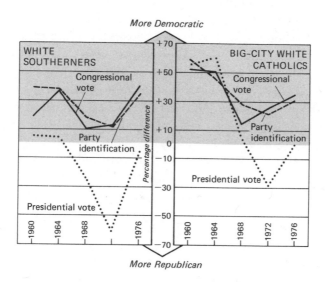

SOURCE: These data are from Gallup surveys made available by the Gallup Organization through the Roper Center.

ern regional pride or loyalty was present, extended by the fact that Carter was the first politician from a Deep South state to win a major-party presidential nomination since Zachary Taylor of Louisiana in 1848. In his religious attachments, ethnic background, and style—he was the first major-party presidential nominee in more than a century who did not "talk with an accent"—Jimmy Carter was part of the southern mainstream. *Yet Jimmy Carter failed to win a majority of the vote among southern whites.*

The New Deal Democratic presidential majority is gone. It will not soon be brought back. The New Liberalism impacts too strongly on the national stage and it is too divisive for the Democrats—however skillful their candidates—to be able to package a ticket that leaves both New Liberals and Old Liberals comfortably allied.

It is no accident—and no small thing, either—that the vulnerability of the presidential Democrats expresses itself far more in defections by less privileged voters than in fall-off among the more privileged. This pattern represents a key feature of American politics in the 1970s: liberalism is being turned upside down. Whereas once upon a time it was the lower economic groups that provided liberalism with its bedrock strength, especially in the presidential arena, now it is increasingly the intellectual and professional groups from the upper economic strata who do. Members of the New Class, while they do not yet dominate the Democratic presidential party, are preoccupied with it and have become a major force within it. For reasons the next chapter takes up, they have far more influence within the presidential party than their numbers alone would suggest. Their influence has tended to alienate the groups who were the prime supporters of the Old Liberalism—the white working and lower middle classes, who are the most strongly opposed to the New Liberalism.

The 1968 presidential election provided the first clear-cut instance of an inversion of the familiar New Deal relationship of class and liberal voting. For the most part, the top of the social order gave stronger backing to the more liberal candidate, Hubert Humphrey, than did the bottom. Humphrey was supported, for example, by 50 percent of young, college-trained whites in professional and managerial jobs, but by just 32 percent of young men and women in semiskilled and unskilled jobs.

This inverted vote pattern became even clearer in 1972, when the somewhat distoring factor of the Wallace candidacy was removed. Among whites in the year of the McGovern debacle, those with college training were more Democratic than those who had not attended college; persons in the professional and managerial stratum were more Democratic than the semiskilled and unskilled work force; and so on. McGovern was backed by 45 percent of the college-educated young, but by only 30 percent of their age mates who had not entered the groves of academe. In 1948, by way of contrast, Truman's support was about 25 percentage points greater among low-status than among high-status voters.

Persons of lower socioeconomic standing were relatively more Democratic, compared with their upper-status counterparts, in the 1976 Carter-Ford race than in either of the two preceding elections. Carter ran a campaign that minimized rather than heightened the "social issue" concerns of lower-status whites. And actual social conditions in 1976 made it far easier for a Democratic nominee to accomplish this than it had been in 1968 and 1972. Still there was no return to the relatively sharp and traditional class divisions of the New Deal years, not even to that of 1960.

A Challenge from the Policy Intellectuals

As the Democrats cope with the strains and ironies of the inversion of liberalism, they must also deal with a couple of challenges from other quarters. One of these emerges out of some new intellectual currents now starting to run in the universities. At the very time the New Deal state has attained acceptance across a very large portion of the American social spectrum, it has come in for increasingly heavy criticism from experts on public policy. This sort of thing has happened before. In the 1920s, for example, when the old Republican public philosophy of industrial nation building and national integration under the aegis of business was at its zenith in mass support, it was being attacked by the policy intellectuals.

The current challenge to the old liberal orthodoxy is at its liveliest in the writings of a loosely knit group of now-dissenting Old Liberals—men such as Aaron Wildavsky, James Q. Wilson, Nathan Glazer, and Senator Daniel Patrick Moynihan —and in their principal journals, *Commentary* and *The Public Interest*. All manner of basic questions are being raised. Hasn't the New Deal state, they ask, been "Balkanized" programmatically, broken into a series of small units, each manipulated by a cluster of special interests? Doesn't governmental regulation, introduced to protect "the people" from "the interests" often serve to advance the interests over the people? Aren't public bureaucracies, by their very size and insulation, inherently unresponsive to popular wishes? Haven't so many government intrusions been fostered as to incapacitate the private economic system in a number of critical areas? Doesn't the secular march of government spending, absolutely, and as a relative slice of the gross national product, expose the United States to the economic disorder known as the "English sickness"? Thus there is among these policy intellectuals a general sense that New Deal liberalism, for all of its accomplishments, may have exhausted itself, that "more of the same" won't work.

The outcome of what is still a disjointed critique of the liberal orthodoxy could eventually be the formulation of a new public philosophy. Should this occur, it would obviously introduce a major force for change in the U.S. party system. But at present, the party balance is little affected. The debate has not penetrated into the mass public. And what is far more important for the long run, the most creative and most rapidly expanding circles of liberal criticism encompass people whose attachments remain to the Democratic party rather than to the Republicans—primarily because the latter seem reactive and backward-looking. The GOP has been routed so thoroughly within the intellectual community that it finds itself confined to a spectator role in the great unfolding debate. The dissenting policy intellectuals—traditional conservatives excepted—don't see any place for themselves to go outside the Democratic camp.

Who Pays the Bill?

A more serious threat to the Democrats-as-majority-almost-everywhere arises out of the fact that lower- to lower-middle-income groups are finding themselves less and less in the position of beneficiaries of domestic social spending programs and more and more in the role of contributors. Total government expenditures, not including defense, have grown at an extraordinary rate over the past two decades—from $49.9 billion in 1954 to $416.2 billion in 1975. This jump has been sustained in part by increases in the effective tax rate—but the increases have not been distributed evenly throughout the population. For families earning incomes around the national median, the rise has been much steeper than for upper-middle- and upper-income families. Those earning four times the median in 1953 —about $20,000—paid 20.2 percent of their income in taxes, while those at the median paid 11.8 percent. Twenty-two years later, median-income families were taxed 22.7 percent of their income, while the rate for those earning four times as much had climbed much more slowly to 29.5 percent.*

Trying to sum up the meaning of these data, journalist David Broder commented that it is "no wonder there is a tax revolt in this country."† It is at least as appropriate to say: no

---

* Advisory Commission on Intergovernmental Relations, *Significant Features of Fiscal Federalism, 1976* (Washington, D.C., June 1976, Part 1), especially p. 40.
† David Broder, *Washington Post*, August 4, 1976.

wonder the liberal political order has been turned upside down. People at the top today do not pay a much higher share of their income in taxes than do those in the lower middle class, even though the better-off have much more of a cushion. The burden of paying for the vast expansion of the role of the state has in a real sense been borne disproportionately by the middle- and lower-middle-income brackets.

A Continuing Contradiction

Thus, it is no surprise to discover that today the young, college-trained professionals of the New Class are more liberal than the older, high school–educated, blue-collar people *even* on issues of social spending. Both, to be sure, favor a high level of expenditures. But the less affluent Democrats are less inclined to favor increased governmental expenditures for health care, for urban problems, for meeting the needs of blacks, and the like, than are their more privileged counterparts.

Clearly there are limits to how far this movement of the middle class from beneficiary to contributor status can go before it produces an authentic bourgeois defection from, and challenge to, the New Deal state. To date no such challenge has developed on a national scale. This is partly because the lower-middle and working classes continue to express strong support for big government even while there has been an exceptional increase in the backing that high-income, high-status groups give to government spending as they gain more and contribute proportionally less. But, again, the lack of a challenge testifies to the absence of an alternate "progressive" public philosophy. The American people are of no mind to simply repudiate the New Deal governmental interventions.

It is likely that the various extensions of liberalism will continue to generate resistance within the enormous middle class of this postindustrial society, and that this resistance will be a special problem for the Democratic presidential party. As the GOP will probably persist in its half-a-party status, so it can be expected that the Democrats will remain a most curious electoral contradiction—a majority party that, partly by default, dominates the sweep of public life but is hard pressed to break even in the most important, visible, and intensely symbolic of offices, the presidency.

CHAPTER 3

☆ ☆ ☆ ☆ ☆ ☆

The Perils of Party Reform

*O*VER THE 1960s AND 1970s THE AMERICAN PARTY SYSTEM
has been performing strangely, yielding novel and all
too often unfortunate results. For instance, in two of the past
four presidential elections—1964 and 1972—the victors were
beneficiaries of two of the greatest landslides in U.S. history.
But the voters did not so much confer mandates on Lyndon
Johnson and Richard Nixon as declare their opponents unac-
ceptable. There is every indication that these negative landslides had adverse consequences for the political order. Large
numbers of people felt they were without a proper choice.

Since 1964, American presidential nomination campaigns
have been distinguished by the frequency of strong candidacies of a decided ideological character. Not popular with the
mass constituencies of their respective parties, Goldwater,
McCarthy, McGovern, and Reagan managed nonetheless either to command the nomination or come within an eyelash of
doing so. And all of this happened at a time when both parties
were implementing a series of momentous reforms designed to
make themselves more representative!

Then, in 1976, with the Republicans at their post-Watergate
nadir and presidential victory available to the opposition vir-

tually for the asking, the Democrats—the American majority party and the oldest political party in the world—brought forth a candidate who was almost completely unknown and untried in national politics. Not more than 3 or 4 percent of the electorate could even identify Jimmy Carter six months before he was nominated for the most important of all offices. It is not surprising that the Carter campaign encountered persisting doubt and skepticism on the part of the public. The voters were dissatisfied with things as they were, but felt quite unsure whether they would be any better off with Carter in the White House. Partly for this reason, Carter's lead in the polls fell precipitously between July and October, and an election that had seemed destined to bring about the decisive retirement of a much-burdened incumbent became instead a near deadlock.

This series of strange electoral performances is chiefly the result of the pronounced weakening of American political parties that has taken place in recent decades—a process that by now has brought them to the point of virtual death as organizations. As a consequence of their increasing weakness, the parties are unable to perform a set of functions which are exclusively theirs, and the whole political system has been rattled.

An American Ambivalence

The enfeeblement of the parties has come to a head during the last decade, a span filled with partisan changes and experimentation that are conventionally billed as "reform." But if reform is understood to mean "the improvement or amendment of what is wrong," little of the sort has occurred. Reform proponents insist that the alterations have made the parties more democratic, more representative of the populace, stronger, more competitive, and generally better able to play their part in the governing process. In fact, the changes seem more to have deformed than reformed the parties. They have left the system on the whole less representative, less competitive, less able to govern.

The organizational weakness of U.S. political parties is in one sense an old story. Though Americans gave the world its first party system, they have always been highly ambivalent about the institution. Party leaders have been seen pejoratively as "bosses" and parties themselves as no better than "necessary evils." This approach to party follows in large measure from the culture's distinctive individualism, which prompts Americans to insist on their individual rights to determine electoral outcomes, and specifically on *their* rights, rather than those of party leaders, to control the nomination process.

The reform movements of the twentieth century, however, have carried the enfeeblement of parties way beyond anything required by the culture. In the early years of this century, the Progressives took a number of critical steps in that direction, particularly through their generally successful advocacy of the idea that nominations for state and local office be controlled by voters who turn out in primaries rather than by the party organization. The capacity of regulars to manage party life was decisively lessened and a theory of intraparty democracy, compatible with the old American emphasis on individual action and the suspicion of large organizations, took root to an extent not found in any other democratic system. The direct primary remains almost exclusively an American institution.

Over the last decade, a new burst of reform activity has picked up where the Progressives left off. It originated largely within the Democratic party, but in a less dramatic fashion it has engulfed the Republicans as well. And it has rendered the two great national parties unable to control the nominating process for the country's most important political office, that of president.

Party Reform since 1968

The current wave of party reform was set in motion by the tumultuous 1968 Democratic convention, which created two commissions, one headed by Senator George McGovern to examine and make recommendations bearing on delegates selection (a commission subsequently chaired by Representative Donald Fraser of Minnesota); the other led by Representative James O'Hara of Michigan to study convention rules and operations. Recommendations of the McGovern-Fraser Commission, implemented for the 1972 convention, proved particularly important and generated rancorous intraparty debate.*

The commission insisted that *internal party democracy* was the primary value to be promoted. The changes which it was able to achieve required the state Democratic parties to "overcome the effects of past discrimination by affirmative steps" to assure the representation of blacks, women, and young people at the national conventions and other party functions "in reasonable relationship to [the group's] presence in the population of the State." Minority views were to be represented in all slate-making sessions. Delegates were to be chosen almost exclusively through caucus and convention arrangements open to all party adherents and providing proportional representation for minority candidates, or through primaries. If a state Democratic party insisted on permitting its central committee to play a role in choosing delegates to the national convention, it was required to limit the number of delegates thus selected to not more than 10 percent of the total. Proscribed was the practice whereby "certain public or Party office holders are delegates to

---

* For the full text of the McGovern-Fraser Commission recommendations, see *Mandate for Reform: A Report of the Commission on Party Structure and Delegate Selection to the Democratic National Committee, 1970.*

county, State, and National Conventions by virtue of their official position." Use of the unit rule—casting a state's delegate votes as a bloc, in the direction desired by the majority— was banned.

Party leaders in many states found the new stipulations involving the "democratized" caucuses and conventions for national delegates selection so complex and so unpalatable—the rules made these bodies available for easy manipulation by candidate supporters or issue enthusiasts and thereby greatly weakened the position of the regular leadership—that they opted instead for presidential primaries. The result was an explosion in the number of primaries, quite unforeseen by most McGovern-Fraser Commission members—from seventeen in 1968 to twenty-three in 1972 to thirty in 1976. Whereas less than half of all delegates to the 1968 conventions were chosen by primaries, nearly three-fourths of the 1976 delegates were thus selected.

Many party regulars called foul in 1972, insisting they had been victimized by a McGovern coup. The de facto quota system for blacks, women, and young people received the most public attention. But in fact it was the general weakening of the capacity of party organization to control the nomination process that was the really consequential change.

Given the massive electoral setback which followed the work of the "reformed" 1972 Democratic convention and a vigorous counterattack by labor and other groups of party regulars, many believe that the 1972 changes in intraparty operation would be compromised away. In fact, they were not.

Two commissions set up by the 1972 convention continued the transformation of party organization and procedures: the Democratic Charter Commission, chaired by Terry Sanford; and the Commission on Delegate Selection and Party Structure, headed by Barbara Mikulski. The 1972 requirements that delegates be selected through open processes (primaries and caucuses) in which any party adherent wishing to participate could do so—at the expense of the influence of party regulars —was sustained. Winner-take-all schemes of delegates selection were banned, with proportional representation required, so that in every stage of the selection process "delegations shall be allocated in a fashion that fairly reflects the expressed presidential preference . . . of the primary voters, or if there be no binding primary, the convention and caucus participants."*

In 1975, Democratic National Chairman Robert Strauss established a commission whose specific assignment was well indicated by its title: The Commission on the Role and Future of Presidential Primaries. Chaired by Morley Winograd of Michigan, the commission found its assignment greatly expanded by the 1976 national convention; it became the Commission on Presidential Nomination and Party Structure, a full-fledged successor to McGovern-Fraser and Mikulski.

The Winograd Commission seems likely to be remembered primarily for reconfirming the victory won by the McGovern reformers six years earlier. *Party* control over presidential nominations is not being revived; instead it has continued to recede.

Indicative of the state of the organizational parties is the fate of an effort by advocates of stronger party control to make all principal Democratic office holders—governors, congressmen, U.S. senators—ex officio convention delegates. The attempt failed to attract as much as one-third support at a crucial September 1977 meeting of the Winograd Commission. Even though more than 200 Democratic members of Congress had signed a letter indicating their strong interest in ex officio delegate status, more than two-thirds of the commission mem-

---

* "Delegate Selection Rules for the 1976 Democratic National Convention," the Democratic National Committee, March 1, 1974.

bers were unpersuaded that a party "elite" should receive such preferential treatment.*

As the Democrats were making these dramatic changes, the Republicans were plodding along in much the same direction. The low-profile Delegates and Organizations (DO) Committee was the GOP counterpart to the McGovern-Fraser Commission, and after the 1972 convention, the Rule 29 Committee continued the Republicans' reform efforts, paralleling the Commission on Delegate Selection and Party Structure (Mikulski Commission), which was then operating within the Democratic party. While obviously the GOP was not so occupied with affirmative-action measures to increase minority representation, it adopted new procedures for delegate selection that are basically the same in their antiparty thrust as those of the Democrats. And even if the Republicans had done nothing along these lines, they still would have felt the effects of reform. Many of the Democrats' changes—particularly the increased use of primaries—have been written into state law and so apply to both parties.

Other Precipitants of Party Decline

Reform has weakened the parties indirectly as well as directly. When nearly three-fourths of all Democratic convention delegates (and more than two-thirds of Republican delegates)

---

* The Winograd Commission held its final meeting on January 21–22, 1978. A set of recommendations to the Democratic National Committee was adopted. The commission did *not* recommend ex officio voting delegate status for the principal Democratic office holders. In a modest bow in this direction, however, it did recommend that each state's delegation to the national convention be increased by 10 percent and that these seats be filled with elected officials and party leaders—with the choice of the latter to be made by each state.

are selected through primaries, for example, serious candidates have to create elaborate personal organizations to wage the costly and far-flung campaigns that are a precondition of winning. The victorious contender, once his nomination is in hand, is hardly about to disband the apparatus he put together for the primary struggle. He relies upon it and not on the party in the general election. Much attention has been devoted to the Committee to Re-elect the President, the now-disgraced instrument of the Nixon forces in 1972. Yet for all its excesses, CREEP was in many ways the prototypical contemporary electoral organization: it was formed to serve the interests of one man; it placed these above the party's; and its substantial resources enabled it to disregard the party in contesting for the presidency.

Broad social changes have also helped to bring parties to the verge of organizational extinction. The populace is much more highly educated than ever, has many more sources of political information, clearly feels less dependent upon party as an active intermediary in the electoral process—and it is sharply and irreversibly more inclined to participate on an independent, nonpartisan basis.

The rise of the national press has also played a part in weakening the parties. Increasingly it has taken over important facets of the communications role that was once performed by party organizations. As journalist David Broder has observed, newsmen now serve as the principal source of information on what candidates are saying and doing. They act the part of talent scouts, conveying the judgment that some contenders are promising, while dismissing others as of no real talent. They also operate as race-callers or handicappers, telling the public how the election contest is going. At times they function as public defenders, bent on exposing what they consider the frailties, duplicities, and sundry inadequacies of a candidate;

and in some instances they even serve as assistant campaign managers, informally advising a candidate, and publicly, if indirectly, promoting his cause.*

With so much going against parties, one might have hoped for a modest dose of "countercyclical policy" to bolster a deteriorating but useful institution. Just the opposite, however, has been happening. For example, federal funding of presidential campaigns, voted into law as a means of "cleaning up" national politics, has reduced the dependency of candidates on party and on the interest groups that have served as prime building blocks of party organization. A number of proposals for further electoral reform now under consideration would have a similar effect. For example, there is strong support these days for a constitutional amendment to eliminate the electoral college and substitute direct election of the president. Whatever the proposal's overall merits, it would reduce the role of state parties by making state boundaries irrelevant to election outcomes. Candidates would become even freer to campaign without regard to the blocs, alliances, and structures that state party systems are built on.

There has been inadvertence and bad planning and just plain stupidity in all of this. But above all, the attack on political parties has come as a result of a straightforward and quite conscious pursuit of group interests. Senator McGovern for one has conceded that there are risks in "democratizing" the party, "opening it up," reducing the domination of "bosses" or "elites," and permitting "the people" to decide who the nominees will be. But he considers the risks to be worth it. "The alternative," he says, "is a closed system where you say the elite are better able to run the country than rank-and-file citizens."†

---

* David S. Broder, "Political Reporters in Presidential Politics," in Charles Peters and Timothy J. Adams (eds.), *Inside the System: A Washington Monthly Reader* (New York: Praeger, 1970), pp. 3–22.
† Interview with U.S. Senator George McGovern, May 9, 1977.

The People Aren't the Winners

McGovern could not be more wrong in his notion that it is "rank-and-file-citizens" who benefit from party "reform" and the elite who suffer; just the opposite is the case. For a century and a half, U.S. political parties, with all their faults, have been a force for extending democracy. Can there ever have been any real doubt that, were party removed from control over presidential nominations and the public invited to fend for itself in a lightly structured selection process, the winners would not be "the people"? In fact, it has been upper-middle-class groups, not the broad mass of Americans, who have confronted the party organizations, who have held them to be unresponsive to their policy perspectives, who have attacked the legitimacy of "bosses," who have urged "democratization." And it is these highly educated, well-informed, relatively prosperous groups who have primarily benefited from party "reform," for they tend to participate in more open nomination processes at a rate that far exceeds that of "rank-and-file-citizens."

That party reform serves the interests of the upper middle class can be seen in the statistics on voter turnout in primary elections. There has been much handwringing of late about low turnout in recent general elections, but participation in them is positively robust compared with that in the primaries. In 1976, for example, in the twenty-eight states that held presidential primaries and kept statewide data on them, just 28 percent of the voting-age population went to the polls, as compared with 54 percent casting presidential ballots from those states in the November election (see Table 1). And there was nothing unusual about this. In the eleven state presidential primaries that were contested within both parties between 1948 and 1968, the average turnout was 39 percent, as against

TABLE 1.

Voter Turnout in the 1976 Presidential Primaries and the General Election

State	Total voting age population	Votes cast in 1976 presidential primaries	Percent turnout: primaries	Votes cast in 1976 presidential election	Percent turnout: election
Alabama	2,501,000	665,855	26.6	1,182,959	47.3
Arkansas	1,458,000	534,341	36.6	767,146	52.6
California	15,227,000	5,709,853	37.5	7,862,182	51.6
Florida	6,131,000	1,910,149	31.2	3,150,500	51.4
Georgia	3,363,000	690,843	20.5	1,466,614	43.6
Idaho	553,000	164,960	29.8	340,932	61.7
Illinois	7,787,000	2,087,807	26.8	4,728,853	60.7
Indiana	3,632,000	1,245,715	34.3	2,222,362	61.2
Kentucky	2,360,000	439,534	18.6	1,167,052	49.5
Maryland	2,884,000	757,717	26.3	1,432,273	49.7
Massachusetts	4,135,000	914,950	22.1	2,546,003	61.6
Michigan	6,192,000	1,771,480	28.6	3,663,890	59.2
Montana	512,000	196,620	38.4	328,734	64.2
Nebraska	1,080,000	395,390	36.6	606,749	56.2
Nevada	419,000	122,991	29.4	201,876	48.2
New Hampshire	569,000	187,312	32.9	339,024	59.6
New Jersey	5,175,000	602,961	11.7	3,014,472	58.3
North Carolina	3,790,000	798,559	21.1	1,678,907	44.3
Ohio	7,397,000	2,083,207	28.2	4,111,873	55.6
Oregon	1,648,000	730,167	44.3	1,029,669	62.5
Pennsylvania	8,476,000	2,183,122	25.8	4,617,971	54.5
Rhode Island	661,000	74,700	11.3	410,514	62.1
South Dakota	469,000	142,748	30.4	300,678	64.1
Tennessee	2,941,000	574,359	19.5	1,476,356	50.2
Texas	8,472,000	1,979,001	23.4	4,071,878	48.1
Vermont	328,000	72,270	22.0	183,902	56.1
West Virginia	1,277,000	528,269	41.4	750,590	58.8
Wisconsin	3,176,000	1,333,373	42.0	2,104,176	66.3
All of the above states	102,613,000	28,898,253	28.2	55,758,135	54.3

SOURCE: The 1976 general election data were computed by the author from U.S. Bureau of the Census Population data and the official 1976 returns. The primary turnout information is taken from Austin Ranney, *Participation in American Presidential Nominations* (Washington, D.C.: American Enterprise Institute, 1977), p. 20.

69 percent in the same states' general elections.* Between 1962 and 1968, the average turnout in gubernatorial and senatorial primaries in states with two-party competition was 28 percent, or less than half the 61 percent for the ensuing general elections.†

Participation in primaries varies sharply according to socio-economic status, with the higher-income and better-educated groups turning out in much greater proportions than other segments of the population. A study of the California primary electorates in 1968 and 1972, for example, showed that college-educated, high-income persons in professional occupations comprised a substantially higher proportion of the primary electorate than of voters turning out in the general elections. Similarly, ethnic minorities were much less represented in the primaries.‡ CBS and the *New York Times* surveyed presidential-primary voters in 1976, as did NBC, and in state after state they found that the participants came disproportionately from the ranks of these overlapping groups: the college-trained, the professional middle class, and those with upper-middle to high income. In New York State, to cite one instance, 41 percent of the Democratic primary electorate held professional or managerial jobs and 30 percent were college graduates—proportions far above those for all New York Democrats.

And when one turns to participation in the "open" caucuses mandated by the current wave of reform, the turnout is even lower and more skewed than in the primaries. Twenty-one

---

* Austin Ranney, "Turnout and Representation in Presidential Primary Elections," *American Political Science Review*, vol. 66 (March 1972), p. 24.

† Ranney, *Curing the Mischief of Faction: Party Reform in America* (Berkeley: University of California Press, 1975), p. 127.

‡ James P. Lengle, "Demographic Representation in California's 1972 and 1968 Democratic Presidential Primaries." Paper prepared for delivery at annual meeting of the American Political Science Association, Chicago, Illinois, September 1976.

states held delegate-selection caucuses in 1976, and the average number of citizens who showed up represented just 1.9 percent of the voting-age population.*

That the slice actually voting in the new open processes is small and demographically unrepresentative does not necessarily mean that the delegates and the nominees they select will be out of step with rank-and-file policy preferences. But the potential for a clash with mass wishes is high.

The 1976 Republican presidential contest provided a striking indication of how vulnerable the parties now are to unrepresentative candidacies. From March through June of that year, Gerald Ford consistently outdistanced Ronald Reagan in popular support among all Republicans and independents by margins of around 2 to 1. According to Louis Harris, for example, Ford led Reagan 60 percent to 40 percent in late February, 66 to 34 in late March, 67 to 33 in May, and 61 to 39 in July.† Yet Ford and Reagan split the primary vote almost evenly. Democratic cross-overs accounted for only a small part of the discrepancy between rank-and-file preferences as described by public opinion polls and the actual primary vote. The main factor was simply that the primary voters were much more conservative than all Republican adherents. The choice of the broad mass of party adherents finally prevailed at the Republican convention, of course, but Ford was bruised by a long seesaw struggle that, if the rank and file of party supporters had had their way, would never have happened.

On the Democratic side, much has been made of George McGovern's success in capturing his party's 1972 nomination in spite of the fact that at no time during the long primary and preconvention struggle was he popular with the rank and file

---

* Ranney, *Participation in American Presidential Nominations, 1976* (Washington, D.C.: American Enterprise Institute, 1977), p. 15.

† *The Harris Report,* March 18, 1976; April 29, 1976; June 3, 1976; and August 2, 1976.

of his own party. The convention that formally nominated McGovern was strikingly unrepresentative of the policy preferences of the mass of Democrats, as a study by Jeane Kirkpatrick so clearly shows.* When he won the nomination, Senator McGovern declared that it was "all the more precious in that it is the gift of the most open political process in our national history." One must note that this "most open political process" produced one of the most unrepresentative outcomes in our national history.

And in 1976 things remained the same in some crucial respects. To be sure, the nominee that year was a man who had clearly established himself during the primary as a centrist, popular with the party's rank and file. Yet the convention itself was as unrepresentative as it had been four years earlier. The delegates may have nominated Carter and done his bidding on the platform and related matters, but they had little in common ideologically with him or the mass of Democrats. They resembled not the rank and file but the New Class—the young, college-educated, professional and managerial groups who have been especially advantaged by the recent recourse to "open" selection mechanisms. They stood far to the left of the rank and file, particularly on the issues of the New Liberalism —such as whether the U.S. should have a softer foreign policy vis-à-vis the Soviet Union, whether defense spending should be cut, and various social and moral questions ranging from abortion to busing.

A Polarization of Activists

Not only have the national parties become more open to the activists—mainly the college-educated—the activists them-

---

* Jeane Kirkpatrick, *The New Presidential Elite* (New York: Russell Sage Foundation and the Twentieth Century Fund, 1976), especially pp. 281–31.

CHART 1.

Attitudes of Democratic Nominating Delegates and Rank and File, 1972

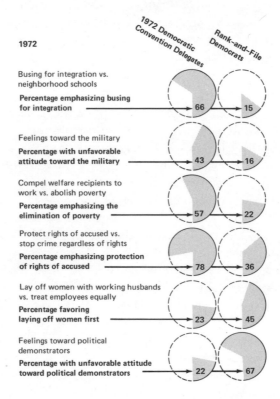

SOURCE: Jeane Kirkpatrick, *The New Presidential Elite*, 1976, pp. 281–31.

CHART 2.

Attitudes of Democratic Nominating Convention Delegates and Rank and File, 1976

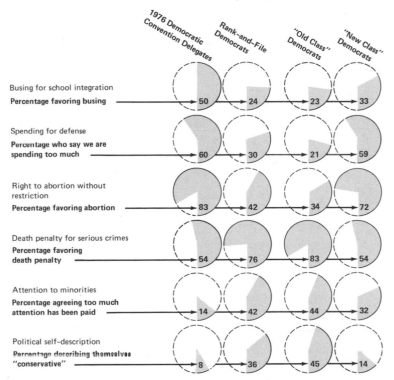

SOURCE: The information on the opinions of delegates are from surveys conducted by CBS News and made available to the author through the courtesy of CBS News. The rank-and-file data are from the combined 1976 Yankelovich surveys and the composite National Opinion Research Center General Social Surveys.

selves have undergone an important transformation. For one thing, their numbers have grown by leaps and bounds, especially because of the expansion of higher education. In the 1930s, 1940s, and 1950s, there was no polarization of college-educated Republicans on the one side and college-trained Democrats on the other. Today, however, college Democrats are noticeably more liberal—especially on the issues of the New Liberalism—than their party's rank and file, while college Republicans are rather consistently more conservative than their party's mass "membership."*

A recent survey by the *Washington Post* demonstrates in striking fashion the pronounced polarization of the activist cohorts of the respective parties, in the absence of any polarization of the ranks and file. The *Post* study showed that Republican party workers, by majorities exeeding 4 to 1, believed that poor people are typically to blame for their poverty, while their Democratic counterparts, by margins of more than 5 to 1, believed the opposite, that the American system is to blame in the sense that it does not give all people an even chance. Republican party workers by more than 3 to 1 maintained that justice is equally administered to all in the U.S.; Democratic party workers assert by a majority exceeding 4 to 1 that justice favors the rich. "The results," Barry Sussman of the *Post* concluded, "almost invariably was a positioning of this kind: at the far left were the Democratic party workers. In the middle were the citizens who identified themselves as Democrats; to the right of them were those who identified themselves as Republicans. At the far right were the Republican party workers."†

If the formal mechanisms of party had not been so abruptly

---

* Ladd and Hadley, *Political Parties and Political Issues: Patterns in Differentiation since the New Deal* (Beverly Hills, Calif.: A Sage Professional Paper, Sage Publications, 1973).

† Barry Sussman, "Electorate More Moderate Than Poles-Apart Party Workers," *Washington Post*, September 27, 1976.

dismantled, they might have provided some barrier to the excessive intrusion of activists representative neither in socioeconomic makeup nor in political preferences of the mass of party adherents. In 1976, for example, Gerald Ford was the choice of a large majority of Republican party leaders and elected officials around the country, just as he was the favorite of the rank and file. The leaders wanted Ford because they concluded that partisan raison d'état required his nomination. He was the incumbent, had not done badly, was well positioned between the main ideological camps, was accepted by a broad spectrum of the electorate, had at least a chance of winning, and almost certainly would not lose badly. If these Republican leaders had still been in charge of candidate selection, Ford would have won the nomination easily.

A Promiscuous Majoritarianism

It is not just by chance that the established leadership was more representative of the GOP rank and file than were the activists who dominated the 1976 delegate-selection process. Party regulars—the leaders of the "organization"—have long been inclined to use what control they have over the nomination process to satisfy mass preferences as among candidates. People who spend their lives within party organizations naturally want to assure the survival and promote the growth of these enterprises, and under the American two-party system, the attainment of those goals depends on the party's success in winning a plurality of the votes in the general election. Thus party leaders and others with strong party ties tend to practice an almost promiscuous majoritarianism that rejects ideological distinctiveness and stresses representation of the tastes of the many.

When one moves outside that small slice of the population

committed to party maintenance, and into the rest of the activists' stratum, the mix of political motivations does not mesh so
easily with the majoritarian ethic. Some of the activists are
strongly wedded to advancing a particular program. Others
articulate the claims of a single interest group. Still others may
be moved by the personal virtues of a particular public figure,
and so on. None of these motives is necessarily incompatible
with majoritarianism: one can respond to any of them and still
devoutly seek to win. But neither is there any necessary link
between the activists' motivations and majoritarianism, as
there is in the case of the party leaders.

The political party as a formal organization has generally
produced representative nominees, not just because its leaders
have a stake in winning, but also because they can do something that mass electorates cannot: *They can plan.* Even if by
some stroke of fate 100 percent of a party's adherents routinely
turned out in a primary, it would by no means be certain that
representative nominees would result. Consider the hypothetical case of an electorate sharply polarized on ethnic lines, with
one ethnic group a 60 percent majority. Add to this hypothetical situation a primary in which nominees for six different
statewide offices are being selected. Given a high level of
ethnic feeling, it is entirely possible that the 60 percent majority would nominate one of its own for each of the offices.
The remaining 40 percent of the party's identifiers would find
themselves shut out.

The situation is not really hypothetical, of course. Political
parties have long confronted this sort of problem and have
developed a fabled institution to meet it—the "balanced
ticket." It is easy to look down on the practice of putting
together a slate with "one Wasp, one Jew, and one Black, one
Italian, one Pole," or some such combination. But the balanced
ticket is in fact a high and eminently sensible form of party
planning. It is a response to the diversity of the electorate and

an effort to put forward a group of nominees who *collectively* represent that electorate.

The public also wants good candidates as well as representative ones—individuals well suited to the complex task of governing. But just as party leaders no longer have the power to assure representative nominees, so are they unable to plan for competence and experience in the choice of presidential nominees. They are, of course, free to contemplate the question of who is the most able, but they cannot assure the implementation of their judgment.

Flea-Market Politics

Thus the U.S. has been reduced in presidential-nominee selection to a system of chaotic individualism. Each individual entrepreneur (the candidate) sets up shop and hawks his wares, i.e., himself. The buyers—the voters—do not find the same choice of merchandise in all the states, and one seller, who may attract only a small segment of all the buyers, is finally granted a monopoly. Candidates are able to win, then, because of crowded fields, low turnouts, and strategic miscalculations by their opponents—but above all because there is no one in charge. Increasingly there is no formal party mechanism in place with substantial authority to plan for the outcomes.

In August 1950, a special committee on political parties of the American Political Science Association brought forth a report calling for a general strengthening of parties in the U.S. The stress of this report, like that of the writings of other advocates of strong parties reaching back to Woodrow Wilson, was on the role the parties play in meeting the public need "for more effective formulation of general policies and programs and for better integration of all of the far-flung activities of

modern government."* Few of the committee's recommendations have been acted upon positively. Today, the American
party system is less able to integrate "all of the far-flung activities of modern government" than was its counterpart of a
quarter-century ago.

For one thing, at the national level, the presidential and the
congressional parties have drifted further apart. In contrast to
the situation that prevailed as recently as two decades ago,
candidates for president now set up their own electoral organizations and go their own way with little regard for, or contact
with, other sections of the party—including, surely, the congressional wing. Few members of the Democratic majority of
the U.S. House and Senate, for example, had anything to do
with the nomination of Jimmy Carter. Most congressional
Democrats now take some satisfaction in the fact that one
bearing their label is ensconced at the other end of Pennsylvania Avenue—but not all that much.

The American system has always provided, of course, for a
formal separation of the executive and the legislature, and this
in turn has made for a separation of the congressional and
presidential parties quite without parallel in parliamentary systems. But in times past, the common bond of involvement in a
party structure that determined presidential nominations
helped to mitigate the rigid constitutional separation. That tie
is gone.

Modern government is an incredibly complex instrument. It
has so many different parts responsive to so many different
interests that the natural centrifugal pressures are well-nigh
irresistible. Party is the one acceptable counteracting centripetal force—and not only at the national level, but in the states
and cities as well.

---

* Committee on Political Parties of the American Political Science Association, "Toward a More Responsible Two-Party System," *American
Political Science Review* (September 1950, supplement), p. 1.

Once upon a time, many American cities were governed by parties. These "machines" surely had their venal aspects, but they were important instruments for integrating and harnessing the strong centrifugal forces at work in the modern metropolis. Not many of these "machines" have managed to survive, but one that carries on is the Democratic party of Chicago—the fabled organization of the late Richard Daley.

"The Best Mayor in America"

It was said of Mayor Daley's Chicago that it was almost unique in being "a city that works."

Senator Daniel Patrick Moynihan of New York, recalling his days as director of the joint Center for Urban Studies of MIT and Harvard during the 1960s, when urban problems had become a major issue, points out that many urbanologists had the highest regard for Daley's accomplishments. For his own part Moynihan says Daley was "the best mayor in America."* This sort of recognition reflected Daley's ability, through the vehicle of the Democratic party, to impose a little order on—and even to inspire a bit of harmony among—the diverse forces of that major city, and thereby to lend some direction and coherence to its governance.

Daley's Chicago had its share of failures. But it seems incontestable that Chicago has been far better governed than, for example, New York, and the reason for this marked difference is party. For the quarter-century of Daley's ascendancy Chi-

---

* Daniel Patrick Moynihan, comments made in a roundtable discussion sponsored by the American Enterprise Institute for Public Policy Research. The roundtable was held at the Capitol Hilton Hotel, Washington, D.C., July 29, 1977, and the text of the remarks was subsequently published by the American Enterprise Institute in a volume entitled *Professors, Politicians, and Public Policy* (Washington, D.C.: American Enterprise Institute, 1977).

cago had coherent party government, whereas New York has been a reformer's dream and a policy nightmare. New York simply has not been governed; the centrifugal forces have overwhelmed the centripetal ones in its policy process.

Political parties as labels, as standards under which candidates run for office, are very much alive and well. There need be no thought of their passing. And there are many who would argue, as does one of President Carter's political aides, that "maybe we don't need parties anymore as intervening actors; maybe in the contemporary situation parties as labels are enough."

The balance of America's political experience with party "reform," however, suggests the contrary. We do need the kinds of services that only strong, autonomous party organizations can provide. By substantially removing party from nominee selection almost everywhere, we have elminated the one institution able to practice political planning. By removing party from governance, we have aided the already strong centrifugal forces working against coherence in public policy. And even in the area of representation, where the reformers have made their proudest claims, it is at least arguable that the machinery of party achieved results superior to those of the putatively more democratic procedures that have been erected in their stead.

Protecting an Endangered Political Species

So it is high time that the nation began rethinking public policy toward the parties. They have become an endangered species, and an all-out campaign ought to be launched to protect and revive them. Direct election of the president should not be established. It would deal too severe a blow to the already tottering state and national party systems. It is possible to take care of the problem of the "faithless elector"—and to remove any real possibility that a candidate without a plurality of the popular vote might win the presidency—within the structure of the electoral college. Federal funding of elections bypasses parties too much and ecnourages autonomous candidacies, and it should be ended. Looking to what are strictly intraparty decisions, the recent proposal by "strong-party" advocates on the Democrats' Winograd Commission to make all Democratic governors, U.S. senators, and congressmen voting delegates to the national conventions by dint of their office should be revived. It is one concrete means of acknowledging and honoring the institutional aspects of party in the presidential-selection process.

The basic change that is needed, though, is simple a renewed appreciation of what useful things parties—as institutions and not just labels—are to have around. If this should somehow come to pass, it would then be relatively easy to rebuild the parties as instruments for planning and representation within what must be recognized as a now-irreversible feature of the U.S. nominee-selection process—the widespread use of direct primaries. Restoring the organized parties to vigorous health and giving them back their central role in the presidential-selection process should be the No. 1 reform objective of the next decade.

☆ ☆ ☆ ☆ ☆ ☆

Postscript

*T*HE YEAR IS 1984 AND THE ADMINISTRATION IS IN DEEP
political trouble. According to Gallup, the president's approval rating has dropped to its all-time low of
thirty-seven. Unemployment has proved to be an intractable
problem, and the president cannot fulfill his promise that
"We will see the inflation rate reduced to ten percent before
my first term ends." With foreign oil leading the way, im-
ports continue to top exports by record margins. "The president," proclaims the *Post*, in language to be echoed by the
other major press commentary, "caught the mood of the nation four years ago, but he has yet to show that he can master
this city [Washington] or govern the nation effectively."

Fourteen candidates enter against the president in the
New Hampshire primary. The "winner," in what is widely
viewed as a "shocking upset" despite the incumbent's political difficulties, is the young governor of Colorado—"Jerry
Brown with skiis," *Time* describes him in the obligatory
cover story which follows his garnering of 19 percent of the
New Hampshire vote.

"All Americans deserve air as pure as Aspen's," the Coloradian argues. "Inner-city kids should have their day at Vail."
Attacking the ever-increasing size and distance of "Washington," he promises to establish a "White House next door" in
each of the fifty states and to spend "at least a few days a
year in every one of them."

After his journey from "the snows of the Rockies to the snows of the White Mountains" culminates in a "big victory," the youthful Colorado governor finds things all downhill. His New Hampshire "victory" is repeated in Florida and Wisconsin. His exuberant campaign workers outnumber and outwork those of his increasingly dispirited rivals. The president announces his withdrawal from the race on Friday, April 13. "Never," *Newsweek* announces in its cover story "The Shrinking of the Presidency," "has an incumbent seen his power crumble so rapidly."

The Coloradian wins the latter primaries with absolute voter majorities, as his opponents bow out and his momentum builds inexorably.

The opposition party convenes in Orlando to confer its nomination on its seventy-four-year-old front-runner—known both affectionately and derisively as "Mr. Right." Drawing upon a cadre of campaign workers at once numerous and enthusiastic, he had "won" New Hampshire in a field of nine with 21 percent of the vote and had developed his own "irresistible momentum down the campaign stretch." In an editorial titled "Last Hurrah for a Neanderthal," the *Times* expresses confidence that "Americans will do what is right. They will reject the politics of the political primitives who are pushing 'Mr. Right' rightward and the country toward disaster."

The president sits out the campaign. He refuses to make an endorsement. Both candidates accept the proposal of Common Cause's Fred Wirtheimer that they run on "meaningful personal credos" rather than "the antiquated institutions of party platforms." Eighty-three members of Congress decline to endorse their parties' presidential nominees. Finally, on November 5, in an election that saw voter turnout drop to an all-time low of 41.2 percent of those of voting age, victory goes to . . .

Predictions concerning American political parties invariably wait upon future elections for their disposition. The party system defines itself around contests for elective office—and especially around the great quadrennial presidential sweepstakes.

This book has tried to describe partisan developments of the present and the recent past, but implicit in its argument is prediction. A deterioration of the capacity of the parties to compete, to represent, and to organize has been detected. No signs of a reversal have been seen. The prediction is evident enough.

Our vision of the upcoming presidential election ends without a glimpse of the ultimate victor. Somehow, though, this omission does not seem to matter much. In the hypothetical scenario, "who" is much less important than "how."

We have now pretty much cut the presidency loose from party. As a result, we are getting, and in all likelihood will continue to get presidential candidates who reflect only fragmented, personalized coalitions of the moment. Largely unprotected by parties, the ultimate victors will be hard pressed to withstand the extraordinary enervating forces which beset the contemporary presidency. Harry Truman won the nomination in 1948, despite his political vulnerability, in large measure because there was such an institution as "the national Democratic party," and that party looked upon Truman as its own. The Truman presidency manifested serious weaknesses and confronted vexing problems, but it proved to be broadly successful—to a considerable extent because of the loyalties and instruments of party that, for example, linked the administration to the Democratic congressional leadership. Such ties, such supports, such checks—for strong parties can restrain as well as bolster—have been substantially removed. The personal, plebicitary character of the presidency has been powerfully extended by the party decline.

The institutional parties are crumbling. That is the decisive electoral fact of our day. Lacking the coalescing bonds that parties once provided, the various units of government will find it harder than ever to pull together toward coherent policy.

The institutional parties have not been some wondrous

good. They have manifested their own fair share of error, dishonesty, and ineptitude. But in the last analysis, they managed to stand in the way of electoral chaos. Today they are a diminished presence. Here, then, is the future which we confront—an increasingly partyless politics that fragments and disorients, and which thereby mocks our effort at mature self-government.

☆ ☆ ☆ ☆ ☆ ☆

Index

activists:
  increase in, 66
  majoritarian ethic and, 68
  polarization of, 63–67
"adversary style," xiv–xv
age groups, Democratic support
  by, 32
American Political Science Association, 69–70

balanced tickets, 68
Before the Fall, 15
Bell, Jim, 19n
big business :
  campaign funds of, 15
  Democratic party and, 15, 17,
    32
  Republican party and, 13, 14,
    15–18
big government, attitudes toward, 27, 48
blacks:

Democratic identification of, 8
Republican party and, 5–8,
  21–22
Bradshaw, Thornton, 18
Brock, William, 16, 21
Broder, David, 47, 57
Bryan Democrats, 14
Buchanan, Patrick, 21, 22
bureaucracies, growth of, 14
Burnham, Walter Dean, 19

Caddell, Patrick, 26
campaign funds, 15–16, 58, 73
Carter, Jimmy, 3, 26, 51, 63
  anti-New Liberal backlash
    and, 40
  black support of, 8
  New Liberalism and, 39, 40,
    43, 45
Carter administration, 17
Catholics, party identification of,
  9, 11, 13
CBS voter survey, 62, 64n

Chicago, government of, 71–72
civil rights issues, 39
  in 1964 election, 8–9
college students:
  party identification of, 11
  see also elites; New Liberalism
Commentary, 46
Commission on Delegate Selection and Party Structure (1972), 54
Commission on Presidential Nomination and Party Structure (1976), 55–56, 73
Commission on the Role and Future of Presidential Primaries (1975), 55
Committee to Re-elect the President (CREEP), 57
competition:
  effect of reform on, 52
  party system and, *xvii–xviii, xxiii*, 32
  by Republican party, 3, 25
  structure necessary for, *xviii*
Congress:
  Democratic strength in, 35
  Republican strength in, 3, 5–8, 12
congressional elections, 32, 34
conservatives:
  increased number of, 26, 27
  in 1976 Republican primaries, 62
  in Republican party, 16, 17, 18–19, 20–21, 23, 26, 66

voting for Democrats by, 27, 33, 34, 40

Dale, Edwin L., Jr., 28n
Daley, Richard, 71–72
Delegates and Organizations (DO) Committee, 56
Democratic Charter Commission, 54
Democratic party:
  activists in, 66–67
  big business and, 15, 17, 32
  black identification with, 8–9
  campaign contributions to, 15
  college student support of, 11
  conservatives voting for, 27, 33, 34, 40
  control of nomination process as issue in, 54
  convention delegates, attitudes of, 64–65
  domination of nonpresidential elections by, 35
  elite groups in, 15
  as "everyone party," 32–33
  expansion of, 27
  identification with, 3, 8–9, 11, 13, 32
  internal democracy issue in, 53–54, 58
  intraparty conflicts of, *xxii*, 27–28, 37–49, 53–56, 62
  liberals in, 26, 33
  lower middle-class identification with, 13
  middle class in, 11
  moderates in, 33

Democratic party (*continued*)
New Deal policies of, 28–31,
32, 45–46, 48
New Liberalism vs. New Deal
liberalism in, 27–28, 37–49
1972 "reformed" convention
of, 54–55
1975 reform commission of, 55
presidential election problems
of, 28, 34–38, 43–45, 49
reforms in, 53–55
"strong-party" advocates in,
73
Winograd Commission of, 55–
56, 73
dissatisfaction:
with leadership, *xiv*, 32
with performance of primary
institutions, *xv–xvi*, *xviii*, 32

education, government spending
for, 29
educational groups, Democratic
support by, 32
Edwards, Mickey, 16
Eisenhower, Dwight D., 1, 19
electoral college, elimination of,
58, 72–73
elites, 13–15, 17–18, 58–59, 61,
63–67
party identification of, 10–11
*Emerging Republican Majority,
The*, 1*n*
establishment:
New Liberalism vs., 39
party identification of, 13–15

ethnic issues and groups, party
identification with, 9, 33
"everyone party," 32
expectations, *xxiii*
frustration of, *xvi*
raising of, *xv*

Federal Election Campaign Act
(1971), 15
federal funding of presidential
campaigns, 58, 73
federal government, public's hos-
tility toward, 26–27
Federalists, *xxii*, 2, 25
Ford, Gerald, 3, 8, 20, 62
Fortune 500, 16, 17
Fortune surveys, 17
Fraser, Donald, 53
Free, Lloyd A., 28*n*
Future of American Politics, The,
10*n*

General Social Surveys (1972–
1977), 29*n*, 33, 64*n*
Glazer, Nathan, 46
Goldwater, Barry, *xxiii*, 1, 34, 50
Goldwater Republicans, 8, 20
government employees, increase
in, 14
government spending, attitudes
toward, 28–31, 34, 47–48
Great Depression, 2

Hadley, Charles D., 33*n*, 66*n*
Harris, Louis, *xiv*, 62
health services, government
spending for, 29
Humphrey, Hubert, 44

income levels, Democratic support by, 32

"independent" voters, 3, 35
    big business as, 17
    college students as, 11
    vs. party choices, 3
    as politically knowledgeable, 57
inflation, 17
intelligentsia, 14, 23, 45–66
    see also elites; New Liberalism

Jeffersonians, 27
Jews, party identification of, 9
Johnson, Lyndon B., 34, 50

Kirkpatrick, Jeane, 63, 64n

labor, organized, campaign funds of, 15
Laxalt, Paul, 2, 11–13, 20
leadership, decline in satisfaction with, xiv, 32
Lesh, Donald R., 28n
liberalism, New Deal vs. New Class, 27–28, 37–38
liberals:
    in Democratic party, 26, 33
    in Republican party, 19, 20
lower middle class, 38–39, 44, 47–48
    party identification of, 11–13, 21
    see also middle class
Lubell, Samuel, 10

McCarthy, Eugene, xxiii, 50
McGovern, George, xxiii, 40, 45, 50, 53, 54, 58, 59, 62–63
McGovern-Fraser Commission, 53, 55
"machine" politics, 71–72
majoritarianism, 67–68
Marusi, Augustine R., 17
Middle Atlantic states, Republican strength in, 5
middle class, 47–48
    myths of, 10–11
    New Liberalism and, 38–39
    party identification of, 9–13
    see also lower middle class; upper middle class
Mikulski, Barbara, 54
moderates:
    in Democratic party, 33
    in Republican party, 16–17
    see also middle class; wage workers
Moynihan, Daniel Patrick, 46, 71
myths, political:
    of middle class, 11–13
    of old establishment, 13–14

"New Class" liberals, see New Liberalism
New Deal, xxii, 13, 17
    liberalism, 23, 27, 37–48
    policies, 28–31, 32, 45–46, 48
New England States, Republican strength in, 5
New Liberalism:
    members of, 37, 40, 44, 45, 48, 63, 66

vs. New Deal liberalism, 37–49

policy intellectuals of, 45–46

New Presidential Elite, The, 63n, 64n

news media:

    effect on high-visibility offices of, 3, 35–36, 57–58

    Nixon administration attacks on, 14–15

Nixon, Richard M., *xxiii*, 1, 8, 50

Nixon administration, 14–15, 17

Northeast states, Republican strength in, 5

1964 elections:

    civil rights issues in, 8

    middle-class voting in, 11

1976 elections:

    business money in, 15

    conservative votes for Democrats in, 34

    party standing in (table), 4

    voter composition and turnout in, 59, 60, 61

    see also presidential elections

O'Hara, James, 53

one-and-one-half-party system, *xxii*, 25, 26

"open" caucuses, 61–62

organization, party system and, *xvii–xxi*, *xxiv*, 52

Packard, Robert W., 22

Participation in American Nominations, 60n

party identification, 2–3, 8–14

party reform:

    beneficiaries of, 58–59

    effects of, 51–52, 55, 56–57, 61–62, 72

    issues in, 53–55, 56, 58, 63

party system :

    ambivalence about, 52

    criteria for success of, *xvii*

    diminishing function of, *xiii*, *xvii*, *xxi*, *xxiv*, 69–70, 76–77

    effect of reforms on, *xxiii*, 57–58, 61–62, 72

    "machines" in, 71–72

    New Deal policies and, 32

    in 1960s and 1970s, 50

    Republican erosion and, 3, 25

    role of, *xvii*, 69–71

    see also political parties

patronage, Republican party and, 19

personal morality issues, 39, 40, 41, 42

Phillips, Kevin P., 1, 11, 13

policy intellectuals, 45–47

political action committees (PACs), 15

political parties:

    activists in, 63–69

    coalitional character of, *xix*

    effects of social change on, 57

    factionalism within, *xviii*

    institutional role of, *xvi*, *xxiv*, 59

    leader's role in, 67–69

    organizing role of, *xx–xxi*, 68–71, 76

political parties (*continued*)
popular control and, *xvi–xx*, 54, 59, 67–69
present status of, *xxi–xxiv*, 76–77
presidential vs. congressional split in, 70
reduced relevancy of, *xxiv*, 35, 51–52, 56, 57–58
strengthening of, 69, 72–73
see also party system
Political Parties and Political Issues, 66n
Polsby, Nelson, 24
Potomac Associates survey, 28–29, 31n
presidency:
plebicitary character of, 76
symbolic importance of, 36, 37, 49
presidential elections:
Democratic party's difficulties in, 28, 34–38, 43–45, 49
direct vs. electoral college, 58, 72–73
effects of reform on, 52, 55, 62–63
federal funding in, 58, 73
negative landslides in, 50
in 1964, 50
in 1968, 44, 53
in 1972, 13, 40, 44–45, 50, 61–62, 64
in 1976, 3, 8, 26, 40, 43, 45, 50–51, 62, 63, 65
party role reduced in, 35, 36
Republican showing in, 3, 5, 8

presidential nominations:
leader's role in, 67–69
as minority choices, *xxiii*, 50
party function in, *xxii–xxiii*, *xxiv*, 69, 72
press, party system and, *xv*, 57–58
primaries, 52, 55, 56–57, 60, 61–62, 68
extension of, 54
socioeconomic status and, 61
Priorities in an Uncertain Economy, 28n, 31n
Progressives, 52
Protestants, party identification of, 9, 11
public confidence:
decrease in, *xiv–xvi*
increased by competitive system, *xviii*
representative system and, *xix*
Public Interest, The, 46
public opinion:
on government intervention, 29
on government spending, 28–31
as hostile to federal government, 26–27
parties as energizing of, *xxi*

quality of life issues, 37, 39, 41

racial issues, 40, 41, 42
Ranney, Austin, *xx–xxi*, 60n
Reagan, Ronald, *xxiii*, 26, 34, 50, 62

Reagan Republicans, 18, 20
representation:
  effect of reform on, 52
  future of, 76
  party system and, *xvii, xviii–xix, xxii, xxiii*, 67–68, 72
  in recent presidential nominations, *xxiii*, 62–63, 67
Republican party:
  activists in, 66–67
  alternative to liberal orthodoxy sought by, 23
  big business and, 13, 14, 15–18
  blacks and, 5–8, 21–22
  campaign funds for, 15–16
  "church" vs. "coalition" image of, 20–21
  college students' support of, 11
  conservatives in, 16, 17, 18–19, 20–21, 23, 26, 62
  downward trend of, 1–8, 24
  as establishment party, 13–15, 18
  ethnic representation in, 9
  geographical strengths of, 5–7
  as "half a party," *xxii*, 49
  identification with, 2–3, 8–13, 17
  intelligentsia and, 14, 23, 47
  intraparty conflict in, 19–24
  leadership of, 21, 67
  liberals in, 19, 20
  lower middle class (petite bourgeoisie) in, 11–12, 21
  middle class and, 1, 9–13
  moderates in, 16–17, 19
  neopopulist reaction in, 18
  vs. New Deal policies, 29
  post–Civil War philosophy of, 23
  progressive opinion and, 22, 23–24
  reforms in, 56, 57
  right wing of, 18–19, 34
  strength in 1940s and 1950s of, 3
  Watergate and, *xiv*, 1, 32
Rhodes, John, 21
Roosevelt, Franklin D., 17
Rossiter, Clinton, 36
Rule 29 Committee, 56

Safire, William, 15
Sanford, Terry, 54
Scammon, Richard, 34
Schweiker, Richard, 20
Sears, John, 20, 25
"service state," *xxii*
sexual attitudes, 39, 40, 41, 42
Smith, J. Brian, 24
social-welfare programs:
  class attitudes toward, 47–48
  by private vs. public sector, 22, 28
South:
  in Carter election, 43
  party identification in, 11, 13
  Republican strength in, 3, 5–7
  rightward tendencies in, 18–19
  as "two-party," 5

state legislatures, party strength
in, 3, 35
Strauss, Robert, 55
Sussman, Barry, 66

Taft, Robert A., 19, 34
Taft, William Howard, 36
taxes, distribution of, 47–48
Taylor, Zachary, 43
television, elections and, 35–36
*Transformations of the American
Party System*, 33n, 39n
Truman, Harry S, 45, 76
two-tier electoral system, 28, 40–
41

upper middle class:
New Liberalism of, 38–39, 44,
45, 48
party reform and, 59
voting by, 59–61

see also middle class
urban problems, 71
government spending on, 29

Vietnam war, *xiv*

wage workers, 38, 40, 44, 45
Democratic support by, 32
vs. New Liberalism, 38–39,
44, 48
Wallace, George, 44
Warner, Rawleigh, Jr., 17
Washington Post survey, 66
Watergate, *xiv*, 1, 32
Wattenberg, Ben J., 34
Whigs, 2, 35
Wildavsky, Aaron, 46
Will, George F., 36
Wilson, James Q., 46
Winograd, Morley, 55